go!

India's Sporting Transformation

Essays by **Rahul Dravid,
Abhinav Bindra,
Pullela Gopichand** & Others

Edited by **Nandan Kamath**
and **Aparna Ravichandran**

EBURY
PRESS

An imprint of Penguin Random House

EBURY PRESS

USA | Canada | UK | Ireland | Australia
New Zealand | India | South Africa | China | Singapore

Ebury Press is part of the Penguin Random House group of companies
whose addresses can be found at global.penguinrandomhouse.com

Published by Penguin Random House India Pvt. Ltd
4th Floor, Capital Tower 1, MG Road,
Gurugram 122 002, Haryana, India

First published in Ebury Press by Penguin Random House India 2019

10 9 8 7 6 5 4 3 2

ISBN 9780143447856

Typeset in Adobe Caslon Pro by Manipal Digital Systems, Manipal
Photo essay by Moses Jesudasan

Printed at Repro India Limited

www.penguin.co.in

To every Indian athlete

who has tried, and failed,

tried, and succeeded,

and, yet, tries again,

for the love of sport

Contents

List of Acronyms

AFC	Asian Football Confederation
AIFF	All India Football Federation
AFI	Athletics Federation of India
BAI	Badminton Association of India
BBC	Bhiwani Boxing Club
BBC	British Broadcasting Corporation
BCCI	Board of Control for Cricket in India
BWF	Badminton World Federation
CBI	Central Bureau of Investigation
CEO	Chief Executive Officer
CII	Confederation of Indian Industry
CRPF	Central Reserve Police Force
CSR	Corporate Social Responsibility
CWG	Commonwealth Games
EME	Electrical and Mechanical Engineers
EPL	English Premier League
FESPIC	Far East and South Pacific Games for the Disabled
FICCI	Federation of Indian Chambers of Commerce and Industry
FIFA	Fédération Internationale de Football Association
FIH	Fédération Internationale de Hockey
FPAI	Football Players' Association of India

FSDL	Football and Sports Development Ltd
HR	Human Resources
HSBC	Hongkong and Shanghai Banking Corporation
IAAF	International Association of Athletics Federations
IAS	Indian Administrative Service
ICC	International Cricket Council
ICL	Indian Cricket League
IIM	Indian Institute of Management
IIT	Indian Institute of Technology
IIT JEE	Indian Institute of Technology Joint Entrance Exam
IOA	Indian Olympic Association
IOC	International Olympic Committee
IOS Sports & Enter-tainment	Infinity Optimal Solutions Pvt. Ltd
IPL	Indian Premier League
ISL	Indian Super League
ISRO	Indian Space Research Organization
IWAS	International Wheelchair and Amputee Sports
KKR	Kolkata Knight Riders
MCOCA	Maharashtra Control of Organised Crime Act
MKRBF	Mary Kom Regional Boxing Foundation
MLB	Major League Baseball
MLS	Major League Soccer
MMA	Mixed Martial Arts
NASDAQ	National Association of Securities Dealers Automated Quotations
NBA	National Basketball Association
NFL	National Football League

NGO	Non-governmental Organization
NHL	National Hockey League
NIS	National Institute of Sports
NITI	National Institution for Transforming India
NRI	Non-Resident Indian
NSDF	National Sports Development Fund
NSF	National Sports Federation
OPEX	Operation Excellence London 2012
PCI	Paralympic Committee of India
PBL	Premier Badminton League
PKL	Pro Kabaddi League
PL	Premier League
PR	Public Relations
PGA	Professional Golfers' Association
PPBA	Prakash Padukone Badminton Academy
PVL	Pro Volleyball League
RTI	Right to Information
SAI	Sports Authority of India
SE Ridge	South Eastern Ridge
SG	Sanspareils Greenlands
STEAM	Science Technology Engineering Analytics and Medicine
TED	Technology, Entertainment and Design
TOPS	Target Olympic Podium Scheme
TRP	Television Rating Point
TWI	Trans World International
UFC	Ultimate Fighting Championship
UPA	United Progressive Alliance
WTA	Women's Tennis Association

Aparna Ravichandran's happiest childhood memories are of the many freezing mornings and white-hot summer afternoons she spent in Jaipur, Rajasthan, training in taekwondo and honing herself into a state of near-superhuman fitness. A few years later, though, having acquired a degree in the German language from Fergusson College, Pune, she found herself dabbling in language services at Robert Bosch India Limited. She then rediscovered the joy of playing and watching sport during her master's year at Loughborough University. Aparna joined GoSports Foundation in 2015, in the ardent hope that her work would help to retain talented Indian athletes in the system, help them go on to unlock their full sporting potential and inspire others to follow in their wake. She fills her spare time with some slow running, bursts of angry writing and largely uninspired cooking.

Introduction

Aparna Ravichandran

In September 2018, GoSports Foundation completed its first decade as a not-for-profit organization working in the realm of Indian sport. Earlier in the year, as we were brainstorming on ways to celebrate this, we discussed the various milestones on our ten-year journey. We realized, in the process, that the larger mosaic of Indian sport was experiencing a coming-of-age of sorts. Belief systems were changing gradually, and a revolution was being perpetrated by the new-age Indian athlete who refused to be told that he or she does not matter on the world stage. For the longest time, athletes had been content with qualifying for the Olympics and, once there, clicking starry-eyed selfies with famous competitors at the Games. This had changed; suddenly, there were high expectations and devastation at failing to make it to the podium. What was going on?

Indian athletes were increasingly beginning to show detractors and naysayers their inherent sporting talents.

This realization delighted our team—we were, after all, a collection of failed athletes, who had dropped out of sports in favour of more secure career paths. Realizing our folly, we had then worked our way sheepishly back into the sports ecosystem. We hoped to play our part in changing the tired, negative script and the language historically used around Indian sport.

'Why do they even bother competing?'

'There's nothing to be gained by pursuing a career in sports. Study hard, get a real job.'

'A nation of more than a billion, and no sporting talent . . .'

These myths were rooted in inertia, and we wanted to provide new material that would dislodge these beliefs from public consciousness.

Examined closely, it was the individual achievements of athletes that stood out, still too few and far between for a country our size. Triumphs were being earned after accomplishing the first task of battling a system domestically; one that still posed far too many obstacles. Dealing with the competition was almost an afterthought. Take a few steps back, however, and patterns worthy of celebration begin to emerge.

These patterns are characterized by individual successes enabled by mini-ecosystems of support. Women athletes playing extremely physical sports, putting sporting glory above domesticity and the pressure to conform to social conventions. A badminton coach churning out champions in his sport, refusing to let what he encountered during his career be the template for the next generation. Cricket—the de facto national sport—shrugging off the fallout of the match-fixing scandal and surging back into public favour with a new and glitzy format. Superstars from a variety of sports emerging from across the country—Baghpat, Guntur, Agartala, Shahabad, Talegaon. Regions better known locally in India for seasonal droughts, coal mining and unhealthy male–female population ratios, now throwing up names that foreign commentators gamely attempt to pronounce. Headlines in the media gradually phasing out lazy, fall-back phrases, such as 'crashed out', 'settled for' and 'disappoints again'.

A contingent of nineteen Paralympic athletes going to Rio and doubling the Olympic haul for India, thereby drawing attention to the (mostly non-existent) setup for disability sport in India. Leagues being launched and evolving, creating a demand for qualified support staff, all the while pushing athletes to the fore as brands in their own right. Small-town India sharing dressing rooms and hotel rooms with products of more mature sporting nations, such as Australia and England. A combination of public and private bodies coming together to form a semblance of a talent funnel. In matters of governance, too, a start has been made, with committees formed, athlete-centric schemes developed, reforms proposed, funds made available.

As we stand today, Indian sport is a fount of possibility—fast-growing in opportunity, slow-moving in delivering results, promising in its chaos. Sports management is a legitimate field of study that imparts knowledge on the business of all levels of sport, and is helping bright-eyed youngsters 'follow their passion' and channel it into specific directions of interest.

Certainly, a lot has moved. Change is visible in the numbers of athletes being sent to represent India at the events that matter, as well as in their overall results there. Slowly but surely, the scope and breadth of change has also expanded. There is an overall sense of optimism, given the positive trend in evidence.

As a tribute to the athletes and others who have been authors and actors in this transformation, we wished to commemorate the sprouting of the various seeds of change that had been planted around us. The next step was easy. We made a wish list of wordsmiths who had covered sports for decades—fans first and foremost—who also happen to have built unparalleled expertise in their particular domains. Much to our delight, they not only jumped on-board the project with alacrity, but also added their unique perspectives to each of the pieces in this book. Our advisers—Abhinav Bindra, Pullela Gopichand and Rahul Dravid—also generously shared nuggets from their fascinating, inspirational journeys.

What has taken shape is a collection of sports writing we hope will enthuse even the most jaded fan of Indian sport. With each essay, we were both delighted and dismayed to note how much more could have been written; then again, we believe the best stories are still under production.

This book is an attempt to share with readers the wave of optimism we feel in our daily work. Those of you who follow scores on mobile devices sitting in office cubicles, exulting at the end of a long workday at replays of stunning cricket shots, dangerous vaults, or mind-bending throws—this book is for you. It is also for anyone else wishing to explore the role sports can play in our society.

As you read these essays, we hope you will relive the moments described, engage with the opinions, marvel at some of the anecdotes and perhaps think about sports and Indian athletes differently. We hope this will also create new fans, breathe new life into existing fandom and encourage every Indian to participate in the national project that is Indian sports.

Being the first Indian to win an individual gold medal at the Olympics (2008 in Beijing), Abhinav Bindra is India's most successful Olympian and a recipient of the Arjuna Award and the Rajiv Gandhi Khel Ratna Award. He is the first and only Indian to have held both the World and Olympic titles at the same time. He now serves on the IOC Athletes' Commission. He is on the advisory board of GoSports Foundation and helps to guide and structure its initiatives for long-term athlete development. He is also grooming the next generation of gifted athletes through the STEAM Scholarship Programme of the Abhinav Bindra Foundation.

1

Building Indian
Sports Champions in India

Abhinav Bindra

Sourcing yak milk, balancing on the top of a pole 40 ft high, using screwdrivers and Allen keys, shaving off a few millimetres on a specially sourced shoe sole, eye-tests and matching sights, excess-baggage payments carrying special equipment, the colour of a wall, the wattage of a bulb, Bollywood movies, the right meal, a mother's love, a father's resolve, a sister's belief, a coach's patience.

What have these motley elements got to do with high performance?

Most often, nothing.

And, as my own journey shows, sometimes it means everything!

Given the type of life I have led over the last twenty years, I won't blame you for believing that I might have some secret recipe for 'being a champion'. But honestly,

I don't. I have experimented with my diet, overcome my fears, tweaked my equipment, modified my environment and surrounded myself with the right mix of people who have challenged and supported me unconditionally.

As you can probably tell, I spent a lot of my time experimenting. Trying to be the best shooter I could be. Ask me how this shooter became an Olympic gold medallist and I will happily tell you my story. I can only hope others will find it interesting.

It is true that I have lived the quest to be perfect on the imperfect day. In doing that, I have sometimes succeeded and most times failed. It has been a journey of ups and downs from day to day, season to season, Olympics to Olympics.

Let me tell you a little about the only subject on which I can call myself an expert—myself!

Twenty-two years of competition, 180 medals, five Olympics, three Olympic finals, one Olympic gold. All of it seems a daze. Until it doesn't.

Looking back, I can now see it all much more clinically and dispassionately. I am no longer a stakeholder in my shooting career. I have exited my investment, as venture capitalists would say. That is my past. And I have a future to think about. But that makes retrospection all the more interesting for me.

I was not a natural athlete. In fact, I was a reluctant sportsperson. Introduced to shooting by my first coach, Colonel Dhillon, I instinctively felt that this was for me. This was something I could see myself doing, making a life of and a career from. For this chance, I navigated my way from dream to reality and built the personal skills that were necessary to win. What do I consider to be the skills that made the difference?

In my early career, I was extremely focused. I was trying all I could to make a name for myself as a young shooter. Inexperience meant that my quest was for perfection, and in my mind, that objective was a stationary target. You can't blame a shooter for that, can you? To my mind, the goal was clear and the 'system' a perfect one. All I needed to do was understand the system and crack the code.

Athens 2004 was a wake-up call. In perhaps the most defining incident of my career, I came à disappointing seventh in the Olympic final after shooting what I thought was the perfect game. Only much later did I find out that the lane position I was allotted had a loose tile underfoot, which reverberated every time I shot. In a game of millimetres, it was amazing that I even hit the target! I went into a depression (literally) after Athens. Months later, I had two obvious choices—one, quit the sport or, two, carry on and accept the incident as a case of 'bad luck'. I chose a third, and it defined me.

I chose the quest for Adaptability—to try to be perfect on the imperfect day. I started training under deliberately imperfect conditions, even installing a loose tile in my home range and practising regularly while standing on it. I trained in low light and under bright lights, adjusted bulbs and added peculiar shadows, painted the walls the same colours as the relevant Olympic ranges. Extreme behaviour perhaps. But it worked for me and even came to my rescue at Rio 2016, when my carefully chosen rifle-sight, through which I focused on the target, broke just a few minutes before my event. I was able to remain composed and made it to fourth. Had I chosen option two after Athens, I would have probably accepted it as fate and given up! Did I ever again encounter a loose tile? Honestly, I don't know, and it was not something I thought about ever again when competing. Adaptability gave me versatility and the ability to not latch on to excuses, external conditions or stimuli. My attitude changed to acceptance of the fact that the only thing within my complete control was my own performance—but I was also ready for all the rest that wasn't!

The second personal attribute I honed was Balance. And 'balance' is a term I use here both literally and figuratively. With respect to my early years as a professional shooter, I will attribute to my parents, early mentors and coaches all that I learnt about balance. About learning the value of an education, of recognizing what sports was doing for me. About attitudes to winning. And to losing. The value of training for its own sake. The value of getting better, and competing. Looking back, I can only feel the deepest appreciation and love for the way they interacted with me, usually without expectation and always giving me the space to make my own mistakes, craft my own journey and own my own results. I shot because I wanted to. As I grew up and became more experienced, balance meant different things and needed a different approach. After my first couple of Olympics, I felt I had mastered my body, found the right muscular tone, weight-transfer routines, shooting jacket. But there was one thing I had not factored in. Change.

But just as everything else fell into shape, my body began to change. The eyesight got a bit worse, the back started feeling the pressure of the years of asymmetric shooting posture and every bit of muscle seemed to need more care and work. The target had moved and now the challenge was actually greater, because I knew that there was indeed an optimal version of me as a shooter, and that the adjustments I now had to make were so minute as to be almost imperceptible. Yet, they were significant. This was a challenge I took on even if it was unwelcome. It opened me to new ways of doing and training, to new ideas; it made me willing to listen and experiment again. Reinvest. Reinvent.

A few months before Rio, I visited a fitness expo in Cologne, Germany, and was introduced to TecnoBody. By this point, I had recognized that the body needs as much refining as the equipment. I had built the skill to tell if my rifle was imbalanced by a gram. With TecnoBody I found a machine that told me the same thing about my body. When I stood on the round metal plate on the stability device, a string of sensors measured the minute oscillations in my body. It told me where my centre of gravity was and which way my body was leaning. It helped me fine-tune my stability with real-time feedback. I found this so incredibly valuable that I bought a portable version for myself. It weighed about 50 kg, and I carried it with me on my travels, using it to awaken my muscles and find my early-morning balance. These things may have only helped with the additional 0.1 in the ultimate score, but as I would later find in Rio, that can be the difference between a medal and nothing.

Similarly, I was made aware that in Germany, it is believed that the misalignment of the upper and lower sides of one's jaw can contribute to biomechanical errors and the misalignment of the body. So I visited a dentist, who X-rayed my jaw and made a splint for me to wear while sleeping and training. A sort of plastic denture. The result was incredible! When I wore the splint, the range of motion in my neck improved by 15–20 degrees, and this helped me perfect my alignment. I wouldn't have believed this until I experienced it. Over my career, I sought balance from many sources and found it in just a few. I learnt that personal balance can come from people, it can come from information, and it can come from equipment. But more on that another time.

Beyond Adaptability and Balance, the third valuable skill (and I deliberately call it a skill) was Hunger. I have often been told that things were easier for me because I had access to funding, infrastructure and supportive parents. While that may have been true functionally, and I am extremely grateful for it, that did not change the amount of work I had to put in to get to my destination. Ultimately, I had to shoot at my target alone. No one else stood with me in that shooting lane. No one else held my rifle or pulled the trigger. When I was a little boy, I was spurred on by seeing my name in the newspapers; as I grew older, it was about achieving my dream of being an Olympian; after Sydney, it was just about the medal;

and post Beijing, it was about looking inward and perfecting my processes to a point where I could retire knowing my journey was complete and that my talent was fully spent. What is distinctive is that at no point before that last shot in Rio did I feel my shooting journey was over. Of course, there were days, and perhaps even weeks and months, when I wanted to think of anything other than shooting. But the enduring hunger always had me aspiring for more, for greater perfection, for better preparation, for new battles to fight and challenges to overcome. This skill was all in the mind. It was a burning personal hunger and it was fostered, encouraged and supported, instead of being belittled, ridiculed or given what is commonly known as a 'reality check'. I knew that my degree of preparation was the only thing that was always within my control. Knowing that all the rest was not kept the hunger burning.

What connects these three things—Adaptability, Balance and Hunger? Put together, these skills helped me shoot in the moment. They helped me make peace with the past and accept its learnings but discard its unwelcome baggage. They also enabled me to remain aware of what the future held, allowing it to beckon politely without making demands. As a result, the moment became mine to own and to encounter. On my own terms. Looking back now, this made all the difference!

You could call my story one of 'high performance'. But what does that term mean when 'winning' is every competitor's goal, especially at World and Olympic levels? The concept of high performance conjures visions of athletes connected to sensors and machines, scientists and nutritionists in labs. Yes, it can be these things, but it is also in the little things, the mundane and the daily. It is about every day of an Olympic cycle. What is happening in the body, what is happening with the mind. Is there adaptability being built, is there balance being maintained and is the fire and the hunger being kept alight and alive?

Simply put, to me high performance was about being able to stay in the moment, letting the body take over, with no interference from the mind. No new thoughts. No thoughts of unattended practices, inadequate equipment, fear of failure, the outcomes of success. Sight, Aim, Trigger. Sight, Aim, Trigger. All body. No mind. No regrets.

I would have loved to train in India and find all that I was looking for locally. Unfortunately, given the nature of my quest, that was not possible simply because the ingredients I was looking for were largely missing at the time. I couldn't make training in India my Plan A; it was always a Plan B. At the same time, I could go abroad for a few weeks, access what I needed elsewhere, but home was home and it was where I wanted to be based. The majority of our athletes face this as well; local training is their preferred Plan A, as is the case for most athletes in the top five or six most successful Olympic nations. However, for Plan A to be rooted locally but still be successful when you are competing with almost 200 countries for that elusive medal, we also need to provide three additional things: culture, information and infrastructure.

By Culture, I mean, as a people that which we aspire for, the messages we give each other. Do we believe and communicate that elite sporting achievement is of societal value, and do we act on these beliefs? Are coaches both inspiring and wise enough to know when it is time to let go of an athlete? Do we have parents who don't throw the education card at every opportunity? The way we live and the language we use. All these elements create cultures and environments, and if we aspire for excellence from our athletes, do we give them the cultural milieu where that is the norm, or at least the aspiration? Do we respect that their careers and achievements may not be linear? Do we give them space to make mistakes, experiment and become the best versions of themselves?

I could have easily been surrounded by people who would have given me a lesson on Indian Olympic history and the apparently obvious limits of possible achievement. Instead, I had an environment with people who challenged me to think more ambitiously, push myself, find my own way and craft my own goals. The contribution of this environment to my success cannot be overstated.

By Information, I mean having access to the best knowledge about coaching, technique, equipment, training and nutrition. These formed the bedrock of my growth as a shooter, and we need this to be ingrained in the system to equalize and level the playing field, before innate talent and the degree of preparedness can take over in contributing to results.

Finally, I am thankful to the world-class Infrastructure and Equipment that I was able to access, and I dream of the day when this will be more ubiquitously available back home, to encourage more youngsters to transition from recreational to elite sport. Making the best of all that is world-class available locally reduces costs, increases the depth of the talent pool and increases competitiveness. All vital factors that play into sustained success on elite stages.

Ultimately, contrary to what some may believe, no self-respecting athlete wants everything on a platter. We are ready to fight, fight to improve, fight to excel. What we hate is fighting the unnecessary battles, of access, choice, knowledge and attitude. Of red tape. I believe those are the changes that will foster a high-performance culture in India.

I am hugely optimistic about Indian sports. I feel like we have a number of the requisite ingredients to be a great sporting nation, and this is being helped along by a significant change in attitudes, in recognition and support of athletic journeys, a commitment to better governance through efforts such as the Sports Code, high-class infrastructure that we are seeing more of, and a commitment to building knowledge. We are resourceful, smart and hard-working as a people, and there is no reason we cannot excel at sports if we put our hearts, and equally, our minds to it.

My own aim is to make sure my gold medal helps others break through, receive support and replicate the achievement. If I am able to facilitate this, then my medal stops being just a piece of metal in a showcase and takes on an active, ongoing life, and this prospect keeps me excited and eager.

I cannot wait for the day more Indian athletes put forth their perfect selves on those imperfect days in 2020, 2024, 2028 and beyond.

Rohit Brijnath admires Lionel Messi, Roger Federer and Olympic athletes who dedicate four years for a single moment. He has been writing on sport for thirty-three years and has covered the Olympics, the Asian Games, cricket World Cups, golf Majors, tennis Grand Slams and written for newspapers in India and Australia and also for the BBC South Asia website. He is currently an assistant sports editor with the *Straits Times* in Singapore, and is the co-author of Abhinav Bindra's book *A Shot at History: My Obsessive Journey to Olympic Gold*. He also believes his one-handed backhand has some potential.

2

Redefining Possibilities for a Nation: The Medal That Taught India to Believe

Rohit Brijnath

*C*an.
     A three-letter word. Has no great personality. Slang for toilet. Painted by Andy Warhol. Worth five points in Scrabble.

Then you look again.

'Can' has muscle. It means to have the ability, the skill, the belief. It's knowing 'how to'. It's having the 'power to'. It's worth more points than you can estimate in competition.

'Can' is what Abhinav Bindra, a straight-shooting species with a sense of irony, helps India with. He's not the first one to dismantle barriers, because even in the 1920s and the 1930s, an army officer called Dhyan Chand and his buddies Leslie Hammond, Feroze Khan and Jaipal Singh

Munda were telling the world that India could do some stick-ball magic.

But Bindra, with the heartbeat of a mortician and the single-mindedness of an assassin, wins India's first individual Olympic gold in 2008, and it should be hung in a sports museum as ribboned proof.

That Indians can.

But to understand 'can', you've got to first meet 'can't'. Got to wander down a century of struggle, or however long it took. Got to remember all the baggage of doubt that athletes had to carry. Got to remember all those who tried, who didn't know better, who got intimidated but fought, who had no history to wear as armour, who lived in an India before Google, when 400-metre training schedules couldn't just be downloaded from the Internet. And so Milkha Singh had to go and meet Charles Jenkins, the best 400-metre runner in the world, at the 1956 Olympics, and through an interpreter, in broken English, ask for his training schedule.

And he got it.

One sultry morning in 2018, Rahul Dravid sat in his garden, as unbending once as the trees that form a canopy, and talked about small things. All the little pieces that make up a culture, that change an athletic people, that bring belief, that create a world of 'can'.

His sons were around. The elder one, Samit, plays cricket and when he wants a bat, he asks for an SG one. Made in India. Meerut, to be precise, in the northern heart of chaotic Uttar Pradesh, where even cricketers from overseas come for their bats. On the surface, this seems inconsequential, but once, bats primarily came from England. Names like Gray-Nicolls and Duncan Fearnley, names you uttered with adequate respect. These were superior bats and thus, by inference, so were their cricketers.

Belief comes in bit parts, like 3000-piece jigsaws fitted together over time. The smallest thing is a valuable piece. Young cricketers in a millennial generation have agents and plan their professional careers, but in an earlier time, a single call from a sponsor had meaning beyond money. 'If Reebok sponsored you,' says Dravid, 'it mattered. It meant they believed in you. It meant, I must be good.'[1]

But till players and teams collect all those pieces, inferiority is an easy coat to wear. 'My God,' Dravid remembers thinking after he saw the exercises the South Africans were doing in the 1990s, 'how far ahead are they?'

'How can we?'

People snigger now, those guys were so *dheela*, so soft, but that wasn't an India of cricketers with designer dark glasses and seven credit cards who walked into English hotels as if they owned them, and actually just might have. This was another India, a less brash one, still finding its confidence, its place, its voice, and so many of us going abroad in the 1980s wore that hesitancy of the untravelled and the unsure, armed with our thin packets of precious traveller's cheques, sambar packets as rescue, uncertain of our accents, asking '*Veg milega?*' (Is vegetarian food available?), clad in clothes a few fashion cycles old, walking by Oxford Street shops in a dazzled daze.

Athletes reflect the society they live in, and in those years, they too were daunted. They'd look at everyone else's fancy equipment, gyms, facilities, coaches, trainers and tracksuits while eating a scientifically approved diet of McDonald's burgers because it was the cheapest place to eat, and they would shrink inside. Confidence all curled up.

How do you beat them if you don't belong?

If sport is played in the mind, then that's also where suspicion of one's own talent rests. Indians anyway weren't conditioned then to voice their ambitions. No one wanted to look too big for the boots they didn't even have. Well, not the nice ones their friends sometimes got from abroad. On the plane to England in 1996 for his first Test tour, Dravid was all freshly shaved enthusiasm, thinking about whether a series could be won, till a senior, carrying the wisdom of the practical, said: 'Let's try and win one Test'.

Remember the Titans (2000, produced by Walt Disney Pictures, Jerry Bruckheimer Films and Technical Black Films) is a movie about the semi-miraculous, this was the real modest world of the Indian athlete. It's not that Asian athletes couldn't win medals at the Commonwealth Games, or score centuries at Lord's, but they were understandably inhibited at crucial times. 'In sport,' explained Dravid, 'the margins are so small that any inferiority is magnified under pressure. And so if things got tough, then we didn't have enough history behind us to show we could do this.'

History has a heft we can't calculate, a weight we can't gauge, an effect that's impossible to estimate. Bindra, at eighteen, goes to America to train at the US Olympic Training Center in Colorado Springs, and his education is not just on stance but on psychology. India had won eight Olympic golds till then, all in hockey; America had over a thousand golds and hundreds of heroes, and it's as if the sporting world existed solely for them to conquer. This place was the Kingdom of Can, and in Bindra's book, *A Shot at History*,[2] he describes this:

> Confidence was like some birthright here and they approached the Games without the cynicism whose fumes athletes are forced to inhale every day in sporting India. The Americans truly believe they are the best, and luckiest, country. They weren't going to the Olympics carrying awe and content just to try, they were going to the Olympics to succeed, make history, be remembered.
>
> It was an adventure, a collective one, and I was awed by the importance they gave to team and the building of it. Great athletes littered the corridors. Hey, here's Apollo Ohno, the legendary skater, there's Matthew Emmons, the to-be Olympic hero, there goes a younger, yet-to-assert-himself Michael Phelps.
>
> Their vitality stunned me and, more importantly, infected me through a sort of osmotic effect. Watch, copy, learn, imbibe. If you train with them, and beat them, the discovery is beautiful and immediate: I can be great, too.

India had some of its own history, some legends, some advance scouts. But no one had won an individual Olympic gold, no path had been cleared, no culture of 'can' created. People used to say, this writer included: one billion people, no individual gold medal? For Indians it was a terrific lament and for outsiders a useful insult, but in truth, in a struggling nation full of hardship, where space was scarce, fields few, coaches rare, sports science in its infancy, academics essential and parents disapproving, how many people could actually play sport and then pursue it competitively? It was always a long way from a billion.

It wasn't just a matter of facilities and insufficient role models but also a lack of perseverance. Indian insecurity often turned to apathy. Back home, people mocked athletes as going to major Games to shop, and it was unfair, cynical, but not altogether untrue. Badminton star Pullela Gopichand, a driven man who might have been a stern, dutiful sergeant major in a previous life, said, in his direct fashion: 'Much of the teams (in the past) were not in tune with what was happening in the world of sport. They were happy to be there, taking photographs and exchanging pins. Tons of people wanted to go to the opening and closing ceremonies and now you have to push people to stay back for the closing ceremony.'[3]

Athletes had earned their way there, but some saw no value greater than participation. Victory—and this was not meaningless—lay in getting there. '5 or 10 per cent then,' said Gopichand, 'actually thought of winning a medal. Now 90 per cent or so are doing all they can to win a medal. Maybe they won't win a medal but everybody's disappointed they didn't.' Once, athletes shrugged after defeat, now they suffer.

Awe needs a few visits to rub off. First time you go to Lord's or Wimbledon, you can be stilled by history. All those boards, those statues, those names, that legend. Second time, you might recognize that even at Lord's, the wickets are only 22 yards apart and the net at Wimbledon is the same height as the one in your local club in Chennai. But once, says Gopichand, athletes hardly travelled, maybe two tournaments a year abroad, maybe four, and it was not enough to find the necessary comfort, to figure out the poster on your wall was no caped hero but just another nervous human. As he put it: 'People idolized them so much, they couldn't beat them.'

But there were always exceptions. Always people such as Sunil Gavaskar, Ramanathan Krishnan, Prakash Padukone, Michael Ferreira, whose desire blunted fear, whose drive overrode insecurity. Who forgets Gavaskar against the West Indies teaching us the difference between height and stature? Who forgets Padukone and his wrist sewn together with silk thread? They didn't fear as much as the others. Why weren't you intimidated, I asked Gopichand, the All England champion in 2001, and he replied: 'I blindly believed I was going to win. I just didn't like losing, it didn't matter who it was. It was personal for me on the court.'

These people are the path-clearers, the road-finders, the courage-givers, the confidence-restorers. This is also who Bindra is.

Forget all those hideous clichés about 'Do it for India', because the athlete can only think about himself. In the pressure of competition, it's hard enough to pull your talent along, let alone carry nations. You don't play with an anthem in your head, but according to the sheet music that is your plan for the day. But when you win, for yourself, for your parents, for your coaches, for those who helped you, the medal becomes an inadvertent gift to your nation. Bindra doesn't gaze at his 2008 Olympic gold medal, and he's not even quite sure where it is most of the time. But the medal is really for India to look at, a circular representation of the journey he's lived and endured for years. A medallion of proof.

An Indian can.

Bindra is not a star, because shooters never are. He is too quiet for a celebrity, too serious to be glib. But he's something more important: he's an evangelist. Not for shooting but for suffering, not for gold medals but for holding a dream tightly in your fist and never letting go. He's a reticent man with a great story who eventually learnt to stand at podiums and tell strangers incredibly honest stories about what he lacked.

Bindra's great gift is to de-mythologize success and divest it of exaggeration. 'Sometimes with a big achievement,' he said, 'there can be an element of aura or excessive admiration that's counter-productive. It lessens the deep desperation to win and the desire to get it for themselves.' He wants to show it's within reach, a real aspiration of imperfect people, not some empty, useless miracle.

When he first began speaking after Beijing 2008, called by schools, conclaves, colleges, corporations, he didn't talk so much about his weaknesses, for he was still a competitive athlete who needed to maintain a strong self-image, and was thus unable to entirely reveal himself. But then, as his career wound down, he started to peel himself away, strip off his skin and show people his full self.

'I talked about my vulnerabilities. I talked about my insecurities. I talked about how I used to be a nervous wreck. I talked about how I was a perfectionist for whom nothing was ever enough,' Bindra said. 'I was like anybody else and I just worked, worked, worked. I persevered.'

Even when he met athletes, he was like this, because his vulnerabilities reassured them. *Oh, wait, he's just like us.* 'I tell them I am an average athlete who won because of bloody-mindedness. If I can do it, there's no reason why you can't do it.'

And as athletes warmed to him, tied to him now by this umbilical cord of shared suffering, they opened up to him and exposed themselves and revealed their doubts, and right there, in the rawness of their discussion, something was being built, something new, something honest, something lasting.

Strange things happen to humans when one of their kind opens a door. It's as if all the awe in a nation is let out. In 1998, legendary South Korean golfer Se Ri Pak, whose father left her at a cemetery at night to learn to handle fear, won the first Women's Golf Major by a South Korean. Since then, thirteen South Korean women have won twenty-three Women's Majors.

Two decades earlier, that head-banded Viking with an aversion to razors at Wimbledon, named Bjorn Borg, brought Swedish impassivity to tennis. He won eleven Grand Slam titles from 1974 to 1981 and spawned myths—was his heart rate really 35?—legends, and a respectful brood of heirs named Mats Wilander, Stefan Edberg, Anders Järryd, Joakim Nyström and Henrik Sundström.

'We saw the success he had,' said Wilander once, 'and we decided to copy his style.'[4] No more needed saying.

In India, roughly 200 shooters took part in the Nationals in the 1990s. Now there are 7000. Let us credit even a small percentage of that growth to Bindra. His influence is hard to measure but it speaks as quietly as he does. It does not reverberate across the Indian landscape as cricketing victory does, but seeps into shooting ranges and the subconscious as he changes Olympic tables, record books, beliefs, dreams. His very ordinariness from the outside—neat fellow with tucked-in shirt, of average height, wearing spectacles, with no evident muscle—is a gift and a human reassurance. No god could look like this.

He is an introverted man who makes himself available, a hideously demanding competitor who is generous with his time, which is how path-breakers must be. Shooters interview him, visit him, ask him about the finals, quiz him on desire, and he talks. A golfer wanted to know about the loneliness of travel, and Bindra, who withstood defeated days in cold European hotels, a sporting desolation that eats at the spirit, spoke to him about enduring.

He's not a holder of secrets but an ambassador of possibility. In 2016, appointed as an Indian Olympic Association goodwill ambassador even as he competed, he wrote a letter to his tribe, wishing athletes, giving them his email address, opening himself up to any queries they may have. Sport is a deeply selfish activity as athletes clamber over each other, looking to training, diet, science and equipment to find that 1 per cent edge that separates them. And yet, the best athletes, especially in nations with no sporting legacy and muscular history, offer their experience to those who follow them.

Athletes feed off each other and borrow confidence. When Bindra was younger, he applauded Rajyavardhan Singh Rathore's shooting silver in the 2004 Athens Olympics; he drew belief from it, but he wanted to surpass it. And that's really the idea of a medal, to use it as a springboard to rise higher. It's the spirit Bindra had—he saw, he wanted.

'There's a kick being the first, but I don't want to be the only one,' he said. He doesn't want to be equalled, he wants to be bettered. And so, one of his favourite stories centres on a shooting trial in 2013, when a fourteen-year-old came into the range wearing an attitude that yelled, 'I don't care who you are or what medal you won, but I want to and I am going to beat you.'

A kid inspired by the Olympic medal but not showing it. A kid wanting to beat Bindra because he had that medal. A kid who knew that to beat Bindra, he'd have to forget about the medal, leave awe in the car park, and behave as if he had 'I can' tattooed in Gothic font on his forehead.

When Bindra tells this story, he's never offended by the kid, only delighted. This is his victory. This is his gift.

Then again, on that day, Bindra won the trial. Beat the young contender. Told him and everyone else the same thing.

Calm down, kid. I still can.

One of India's best-known social commentators and advertising and marketing professionals, Santosh Desai is a columnist with several prominent publications. He writes extensively on media, popular culture, consumer markets and everyday life. He heads Future Brands, a branding services and consulting company, and was earlier the president of McCann Erickson India. Desai is a graduate in economics and a postgraduate in management from IIM Ahmedabad.

3

Two Cheers for Brand Sport

Santosh Desai

Something fundamental is changing when it comes to sports in India. After decades of lamenting the abysmal performance of the country on any international level, we can spot the signs of change, as the realm of sport slowly shakes off its torpid lethargy and awakens to new possibilities. A new set of sporting heroes has emerged in the last few years, and hearteningly, these new champions come from a wide cross section of sports. More importantly, sport as a brand is undergoing a gradual but decisive transformation.

It is not as if India's performance in the global arena has improved dramatically. It does well at the Commonwealth Games, has started showing some improvement in the Asiads, and while at the Olympics, the Indian showing is getting better, it is still far from being any kind of a player in the overall scheme of things. But numbers do not capture the full story.

Historically, sport in India has been viewed as a form of leakage of capacity and intent. The time spent on sporting activity was time spent not doing something more meaningful. Devoting time and energy to sport was in effect drainage of potential; time and attention paid elsewhere would be deemed to pay richer dividends. The division between notions of work and play were firmly etched out, and sport, no matter how seriously pursued, was nevertheless seen as a form of play. Rationally, too, given the fact that sports as a career was a very high-risk choice, one in which being successful was no guarantee of being able to make a half-decent living.

Apart from the more proximate reasons for not pursuing sports, there was a deeper cultural one. The idea of engaging in sweaty physical activity was seen to be a lower-order pursuit. What was valorised were the preoccupations that involved the upper body. The mind and its exertions were exalted, and there was a strong class connotation attached to things physical. It is no surprise that the one game that Indians follow the most is cricket, which involves very little actual exertion. It is instructive that, even within cricket, there existed a clear hierarchy that aligned with class—batting, which involved the application of the wrist and needed timing more than strength, was looked up to the most, followed by bowling, which at least for the few fast bowlers India could boast of, involved considerable physical exertion. Fielding came last, and in the days when aristocrats were part of the team, they would send in a substitute and not bother turning up on the field at all.

Hockey, which was the premier sport in India, gradually faded in importance. Part of the reason was cultural—as spectators and consumers of sports, we gravitated to a less sweaty spectacle. Cricket filled time, both in terms of watching as well as discussion. It attracted money, particularly after the 1983 World Cup victory, and a virtuous cycle of greater interest, better performance, more money, greater incentive to become a cricketer kicked in. Hockey, on the other hand, felt like a disappointing memory, a reminder of the time when India excelled, with the accompanying knowledge that this glory resided strictly in the past. The game of hockey had changed in character, and post the arrival of the astro-turf, the Indian lack of athleticism caught up with the team.

If hockey went into decline, the condition of other sports was even worse. Barring the odd individual champions who emerged entirely on their own steam, the state of sports in India was a story of continuous and concentrated neglect. Sporting federations across different sports displayed the same craven need for power, combined with a callous disregard for the sportsperson. The people charged with the responsibility of promoting sports have traditionally been the single-most important reason for the state that sport has languished in. We know this well, and if sport has started doing better today, it has, in most cases, happened *in spite of* these bodies and not *because of* them.

What has changed, then?

Several factors seem to be coming together to bring about a slow but fundamental change in attitudes towards sport. Simultaneously, an environment more conducive to the development of sport is stirring awake, thanks to the efforts of private players as well as some action on the part of the state.

To begin with, there are many more heroes to emulate across many more sports. It is difficult to overstate the importance of this factor. Nothing galvanizes interest in sport more than the emergence of performers we can be proud of. The need for symbols of nationalistic pride has grown dramatically, and there is only so much that can be extracted from cricket, although it may not always seem so.

Sport has become a key marker of nationalistic pride and the market for nationalism is growing in interesting new ways. The need to display patriotism, to consume it visibly, in an overtly performative way, is a new movement that we see all around us. Fanned by the dominant politics of the day, and supported even by key actions of the judiciary (making standing for the national anthem compulsory before a movie screening), aggressive displays of nationalism have become an important instrument of identity today. As traditional sources of identity get deployed less frequently in everyday life, the use of the nation state in a more self-conscious way as a source of identity is on the rise. We are more conscious of being Indian, and we need to show this in many ways. As it turns out, there aren't too many ways available to us, and sport becomes the primary vehicle for carrying these sentiments.

Faces are painted, bodies start hosting the national colours, flags are waved, slogans are chanted, all seething with nationalistic pride in the backdrop of a sport. Every act that validates national pride gets celebrated. Any sportsperson who enables this feeling, regardless of what sport she/he plays, gets appropriated in this quest to prove the greatness of the country.

If nationalism is one pillar that supports a new engagement with sport, the market is another. Consumption needs hangers, it needs vehicles to get its message across. With growing affluence, and the emergence of a new experience of surplus, come newer leisure pursuits. Consumption needs pipelines of attention, channels that connect it directly to the desires of people. As the engagement with sport increases, it starts becoming a powerful way to get to people's hearts and wallets. Commerce develops a vested interest in sport. It begins by exploiting the attention that exists.

Cricket, the dominant sport in India, becomes the first port of call. Money starts moving there, its stars start endorsing brands and every element in the mix gets a commercial value attached to it. Equipment, advertising on the ground, TV rights and so on. It then scales up this interest so as to weaponize it. It converts interest into property. The Indian Premier League is a new kind of asset created that becomes a self-sustaining ecosystem that connects viewers, players, advertisers and investors in an upward spiral of commercial gain. The players earn more, viewer facilities improve and investment in training, fitness and rehabilitation all becomes more professional; it then looks to create new centres of attention, attempting to replicate the success of cricket with other sports.

What a spectacle such as the IPL manages to do is relocate sport in the arena of spectacular consumption. The sport itself is sliced and honed so as to deliver maximum viewer reward—every moment delivers some gratification. The short format, the cheerleaders, the auctions, the patented war cries, the commentators who become performers, the glamour on display, the merchandise, the advertising—the list of monetizable elements is a very long one.

The IPL has become a template for other sports. The idea of repackaging sport so as to heighten its delivery of adrenaline and dopamine is catching on. Kabaddi is a great example of how the market can completely reimagine an old sport. On the face of it, tennis, badminton, hockey and football all had a better chance of becoming more commercially viable. It is a tribute to the imagination of some investors that kabaddi became the next big-league sport. The fact that a kabaddi player could get a crore or more in an auction simply boggles the mind.

While not all leagues modelled on the IPL have become instantly successful, what they have succeeded in doing is opening up the possibilities with every sport. Promoting a not-yet-popular sport is otherwise extremely difficult, for without heroes, the sport does not become popular, and unless it is popular, it does not invite professional participation, given the traditionally sports-averse nature of the Indian. The sport stays mired in a low-resource, low-performance, low-enabling infrastructure space. Today, with the infusion of capital from commercial players who see an opportunity to 'own' a sport, this is changing. Cricket and kabaddi show how money can be made by creating properties from the ground upwards—in the case of kabaddi, without even having to wait for a sport to become big before moving in to exploit it.

The brand endorsements don't hurt either. Brands need celebrities, for they are guaranteed attention magnets. As brands strive to get noticed in an increasingly competitive space, and as entertainment options multiply, they need the help of celebrities of all kinds to associate with. In India, celebrities are in short supply. After Bollywood, sport becomes the arena which manufactures celebrities regularly. Unlike the glamour-soaked ways of Bollywood, sport tends to throw up less-exalted names, but there is a growing market for these emerging champions. Not everyone is a Sachin Tendulkar, a Virat Kohli or even a Saina Nehwal or a P.V. Sindhu, but here too, a door has opened. The advantage with sport is that, unlike Bollywood, here the heroes feel much more real. Sporting achievement makes for great storytelling, for that is sport's purpose—to inspire us with tales of ordinary people fighting impossible odds to perform at a level the rest of us can only dream of, and to win symbolic victories that we can all savour as our own. This makes for a great synergy with corporate myth-making. And that's how business has found and will continue to find uses for sports and sportspersons from here on.

The interest that the market shows in sport has other consequences. For the first time, the air of makeshift clumsiness that surrounded most sporting events is giving way to a slicker, more modern sense of choreographed productions. This may seem to be a minor factor, but it plays a big role in removing the air of abjectness that had become part and parcel of sport. The equipment has improved, the uniforms look better, and while one must be careful not to overstate the change that has taken place—for the dominant reality of Indian sports is still quite grim—these changes do serve to make sport a more desirable option not only to watch but also to participate in.

Overall, the rise of spectatorship is a phenomenon to take note of. As consumers of spectacles, we are hungry for more stimulation. With the increased access to data on our mobile phones, we are now open to being entertained all the time. We are now individual consumers, and the market for content has exploded—every single family television screen has, in effect, become five. Sporting content has a special quality in that it is a reality show like no other. Everything is live and authentic, and compels emotional participation. One cannot watch a game, whatever it might be and whoever might be playing, without picking a side and rooting with unreasonable passion for it. Spectatorship itself may be passive, but the enthusiasm it generates translates easily into more money for the sport and for greater participation in it.

For many parts of India, aspirations do not have vehicles that can provide transportation. As sport starts becoming a little more remunerative, it can legitimately become a mobility vehicle. In a scenario where access to higher education is either difficult or expensive, and jobs are scarce, sport becomes an important source of advancement. In a larger sense, we see a greater openness to mobility vehicles other than education, which was otherwise in India virtually the only way in which people had a shot at changing their life scripts. Today, the idea of talent is seen as an alchemic force that lies within, and which, when properly harnessed, unleashes destinations not possible to reach using conventional means. While talent can take many forms, sport is an exceedingly important one. Stories of sportspersons coming from extremely humble backgrounds and finding avenues to stardom and money are inspiring, and encourage many others to take up sport more competitively. Of course, since today the gap in terms of rewards between those who make it to the top level and those who do not is so acute, it becomes important to find ways to ensure that serious athletes, even if not top-level champions, have the opportunities they need to make a good living.

The third significant factor in the new culture surrounding sport lies outside of it. The traditional ideas of success are slowly beginning to change. From a time when success was about moving up on a single material axis, things are changing. Studying hard and avoiding distractions, including sports and other extracurricular activities (the phrase itself is revelatory, for it makes 'curricular' a default life choice), getting good marks to become a doctor, engineer or IAS officer, getting a good secure job with a multinational company or the government, and then gradually working up the ladder, in the meantime starting a family and ensuring that one's children go through the same process—this was the meaning of a successful life. Today, while this mental model essentially continues to hold, the definition of success has started to become more horizontal in nature. The focus is not only on what you become, but who you become. The individual today is increasingly known by his/her interests and not only by his/her designation. On social media, people describe themselves not by their occupations but by a host of other descriptors—their hobbies, desires, opinions, life goals, pet peeves. Just take a look at Twitter bios—the self-descriptions are expansive and adventurous.

In this context, interest in sport takes on a new dimension. It becomes synonymous with an expanded view of life. As parts of India start experiencing a feeling of surplus, leisure pursuits gain in importance. The focus remains not only on how to earn money, but on how to spend it. Time takes on a new quality. Free time needs to be occupied meaningfully. The need for lives to be adrenalized, for every minute to deliver some gratification, becomes more urgent.

Fuelling this is another big shift that is taking place. The body is being experienced as an important site of change. The biggest changes are taking place in and around the body, for it is the primary asset that we own. In an earlier time, we thought of the body as a given and largely outside our control. We had a passive relationship with our bodies, something that has changed at a fundamental level. We increasingly think of our bodies as malleable and within our control. We can shape them, mould them as per our need, protect them, and use them to extract more life. This body-consciousness has to do with both external appearance and internal health, and is resulting in a new consciousness about fitness that one can see all around. Gyms have cropped up everywhere; in the smallest town, it is not uncommon to come across facilities that are surprisingly well equipped.

The success of marathons is a startling example of how widespread this movement is. People young and old have taken to running with an intensity that an India of yesterday would be dumbfounded by. As the idea of physical exercise begins to become enshrined in our lives, the relationship with sport changes dramatically. We think of physical exertion as a necessary part of our lives, and are happy to encourage our loved ones to pursue such activities. An interest in the body and a comfort with physical activity are the foundations on which a culture more accepting of sport is built.

Far from the arena of competitive sport, fitness has started becoming a competitive activity. Peer group pressure is creating a push towards greater participation. Maintaining youthfulness is now a social responsibility, for it has many stakeholders and several sources of pressure. Age has different connotations today—a fifty-year-old of today bears little resemblance to one from a generation ago.

An important constituent of this change is the increased participation of women in sport. Some of India's most significant successes in recent times have come from women. What is heartening is that a lot of these athletes come from parts of India that are either not the most women-friendly or have been marginalized for one reason or another. The impact that sport has on the lives of women is particularly profound, for it opens up avenues that could not have been dreamt of otherwise.

Sport as a brand has come a long way, even as there is a much longer way to go. The good news is that this change is deep and ecological in nature, as it is the product of many large forces working together, rather than being the outcome of any one dramatic initiative. Because it is organic in nature, it is inexorable in its trajectory, and will force recalcitrant elements in the sporting ecosystem to change. The state's attitude is beginning to change, and the private sector is also coming to the fore.

Much more needs to change, and this book is part of the many efforts to harness the natural momentum that sport has acquired and to convert this into a movement that is unstoppable. For the first time, it does seem that this is not an impossible dream.

Sharda Ugra is senior editor for ESPNcricinfo.com, the world's biggest independent single-sports website and ESPN. in, ESPN's multisport website focused on India. A sports journalist for almost thirty years, she worked with Mumbai tabloid *Mid-Day*, national daily *The Hindu* and *India Today* magazine before joining ESPN. She has written and spoken about issues surrounding Indian sport in academic and popular publications, at home and abroad. She worked with former New Zealand captain John Wright on *John Wright's Indian Summers*, his memoirs of his years coaching India, and with Yuvraj Singh on *The Test of My Life*, an account of his diagnosis and recovery from cancer. She was a fellow of the Australia India Institute, University of Melbourne, in 2013.

4

Storytelling in Indian Sport

Sharda Ugra

Mid-July 2018, when this chapter was way past its many deadlines, an exchange around Indian sport on social media became, to use mobile app language, a notification for our times. 'Our' here is Indian sport—that baffling, exhilarating, frustrating, impossibly optimistic entity—and the Twitter exchange around it indicated that some straitjacketed conventions had been pulled apart.

It took place just after Hima Das kicked in her afterburner across the straight in the 400-metre final at the IAAF World U20 Championships (also called the World Junior Championships), becoming the first Indian to win a track gold medal at a world event. After her successful semi-final run, the Athletics Federation of India (AFI) had commented on a video clip of Das's trackside interview on its Twitter handle saying, '#HimaDas speking to media after her SF win at #iaaftampere2018 @iaaforg Not so fluent in English but she gave her best there too. So proud of u #HimaDas Keep rocking & yeah, try ur best in final! [sic]!'[1]

After the gold, the AFI Twitter handle was pelted by a hailstorm of censure for commenting on Hima's English. The ruling body of Indian track and field athletics was called a 'loser' and hauled up with responses of 'shame', 'disgusting', told that they should concentrate on finding talent rather than teaching English, and accused, among other things, of trying to 'belittle her glory'. To such a degree of ferocity, that the AFI had to apologize on the social network service, doing so in Hindi. A rough translation of the apology read, 'We merely wanted to show that Hima is fearless, whether on the track or outside. Despite being from a small village, she spoke freely with the foreign media. We apologize again to those who were angry.'[2]

Apologies, it must be pointed out, do not come easily to sports federations in India. That would mean the admission of an error and accountability to someone other than themselves. That doesn't happen enough—neither the governors of an Indian sport admitting errors, nor feeling the need to be accountable. While the AFI's Hindi version of an apology sounded more sardonic than heartfelt, there was no denying that the ruling body had been stung by the very public backlash.

Ten years ago, no Indian athlete, particularly one from outside cricket, would have found such a public outcry against their treatment by their sports federation. What was remarkable about the furore over Hima Das and her fluency in English was that the support came from an unknown multitude. They pounced upon the AFI's condescension and turned the narrative in a previously unexpected direction. Rather than Hima being conscious of her English from now on (the athlete herself said she wasn't offended, and admitted, in an interview to *India Today*, that her English 'isn't that good'), the people behind the AFI's social media handles were put on guard. What used to be the modus operandi around Indian athletes (those outside the cricketosphere) in the hands of those above them in the hierarchy of authority is now off-limits.

In a decade of seismic changes in Indian sport— in the breadth of competition, range of success, elite athlete management and the variety of journalism—the involvement of the general public in an otherwise quiet world has been visible and, in many cases, such as Hima Das's, loudly heard.

Until around the early years of the twenty-first century, larger India paid attention to these athletes once every two years—when either an Olympic Games or an Asian Games came along. They were recognized and feted by their sporting community and the media working around it, but not the masses, nor the country's business community.

Other than a few engaging, and it must be emphasized, English-speaking, personalities—such as Indian tennis player Leander Paes, chess maestro Viswanathan Anand, and the snooker and billiards men Michael Ferreira and Geet Sethi through the 1990s—the rest tended to be clumped together under a category considered uncool. The English-language press and media largely fed this general trend, and while they did not have the weight of readership or viewership numbers, they controlled the attention of the corporate cash-dispensers available to sport.

In a conversation about picking a cover photograph for a national news magazine, the image of Indian hockey's inspirational, inflammable Dhanraj Pillay in a resplendent turban was turned down because he looked like a *gavaar* (a yokel),[3] and it wouldn't go down well with the magazine's English-speaking readership. The fact that the majority of athletes fundamentally came from either rural or working-class backgrounds and homes of scarce financial means in many ways controlled how their lives and stories were told to the rest of India.

At that time, communication also travelled in a straight line—from the sport via the journalist/reporter/writer/television reporter to the reader/viewer, with the athlete's voice often found at the far end of it. Sports media until the mid-1990s was made up of newspapers and magazines, and stories about an athlete's success or struggle could only be found there. Information about the athlete without English, at the very start, came from their coaches or the officials who had a grip on the futures of both athlete and coach.

Athletes who wanted to tell their own stories were often considered difficult and troublesome. In a team sport, such as hockey, it was the tempestuous Pillay or goalkeeper Ashish Ballal. Amongst individual athletes, it is hard to name anyone who spoke even little English and protested against or questioned authority through the early 1990s. Michael Ferreira never held back with his English and the one exception to all rules was Prakash Padukone, who led a rebellion against the Badminton Association of India in 1997. Success in an individual sport could provide an athlete some attention and leverage, but it tended to be limited. The athlete as a free agent was a concept that did not exist in India at the time—it is only being recognized today.

The tribe of mostly independent individual athletes was to be found in tennis, motor sport or golf—Leander Paes turned pro in 1991, Narain Karthikeyan's first racing season in the UK was in 1993, Jeev Milkha Singh set out on the European tour in 1998. The rest of the athletes, however, stayed connected within the official superstructure that Indian sport is built around. This meant that government funding and official approval became the underlying basis of their career paths. Athletes were seen, but rarely did we hear them. Never mind rocking the boat, even suddenly standing up on deck was not recommended.

~

When I entered the profession in 1989 and worked out of what was then called Bombay, the earliest narrative spun out (in sports other than cricket, tennis, snooker and billiards) presented the Indian athlete as a creature of deficit. Of means, ambition, talent and that oldest of Indian chestnuts, killer instinct. The coverage of Olympic sport, be it hockey with its ceaseless coach-clique dramas, or athletics with its blaze-and-fade pattern, or any other sport with its narrow-misses, remained one of patronizing tolerance. Wire services and newspapers fed into, and still do, headlines that ran on a rote-cycle of 'X surges ahead' or 'X crashes out'. It was dismissive, clichéd and devoid of detail.

I remembered Geet Sethi talking about his experience as part of the Indian contingent to the 1998 Asian Games. It was the first time Sethi, an urbane management graduate from Ahmedabad, travelled to a multidiscipline event, and he remembers being witness to what he called the 'conscious attempt to stamp out the dignity of the Indian athlete'.[4] It was carried out through an indifference to the athletes' requirements or timetables, the athlete-to-official ratio and the treatment meted out to the competitors by the officials themselves. Never mind remembering an athlete's name, Sethi got tossed a T-shirt as a throwaway 'souvenir' as the contingent's tracksuits had not arrived on time.

At the first Olympics I covered as a journalist, Athens 2004, it appeared as if the media too played its own unconscious part in mocking the athlete. I was to experience first-hand what the effects of that mindset felt like to an athlete. On the first day of the Games, Suma Shirur made the final of the 10-metre air rifle, only the second Indian to enter an Olympic shooting final. From a qualifying field of 44, Suma finished amongst the top eight. Anjali Bhagwat (the first Indian shooter to qualify for an Olympics in Sydney 2000, finishing seventh) suffered a shock exit from qualification in Athens. I remember Anjali sitting with her husband Mandar on the sidelines of the shooting range, after the qualification rounds, distraught. Her hands were shaking. In the Athens final, Shirur had finished eighth.

What the newspapers carried the next day off wire-service reports read, 'Suma finishes last.'[5] When I saw Shirur a day or so later at the hockey arena, I wanted to interview her about her experience in an Olympic final. She was furious. 'Suma finishes last' was a whiplash to her spirit. To her, the media had downgraded her achievement in making an Olympic final, demeaned the effort it had taken to get there, and she wasn't going to waste time talking to us. As the lone representative of the media, I had no defence to offer. Not even by expressing my horrified disapproval of the headline and the otherwise good intentions, so I sheepishly walked away.

Close to a fortnight later, Anju Bobby George broke her national record in the long jump final, and when we stopped her to chat in the mixed zone, she said, 'I am sorry. Please tell everyone.' Anju was the country's foremost track and field athlete: she had won India its first medal at the athletics world championship (a long jump bronze in Paris 2003), was an Asian Games gold medallist and, on the biggest night of her career, had gone further than she ever had before. What was there to be sorry about? Producing a personal best? But we knew what it was about, and it felt miserable. It was the opposite of entitlement, the extra layer it seemed Indian athletes were instinctively made to wear—to be beholden. That they owed us something. It felt wrong.

Four years later, in Beijing 2008, a wire service report flashed a piece of news that wrestler Sushil Kumar had 'crashed out'. The wireman was unaware of the introduction of the repêchage into the Olympics for the first time. After a short break that followed his 'crashing out', Sushil was to win three bouts in seventy minutes and India's first medal in wrestling after fifty-six years. This unexpected bronze—the first time India won more than one individual medal at an Olympic Games—in hindsight, looked like the fates were involved in an unconscious act of defiance against Indian sports' formulaic narrative. *Pay attention, do your homework*, the athlete said, *no longer can we be considered supplicant to your story of our story.*

Beijing had also brought India its first Olympic individual gold—Abhinav Bindra in the 10-metre air rifle. Bindra's gold was to break the barrier created by history and circumstance of what was considered possible, achievable and available in Indian sport. Every athlete from then on found the only standard that mattered to them.

The media, however, took just a little while longer to catch up. On 9 August 2012, multiple editions of the *Times of India*, which should be available currently in its e-paper editions, treated Vikas Gowda's performance in the final of the men's discus at the 2012 London Olympics with this headline—'Gowda ends lowly eighth'.[6] And this was being said of the first appearance by an Indian man in an Olympic athletics final in thirty-six years, after Sriram Singh (Montreal, 1976, 800 metres). Gowda was eighth out of twelve finalists, and had been deemed lowly. On television, during the London Games, an Olympic 'expert' referred to a national hockey player as a 'joker'.

It was one of the last times that the mainstream media, to which I belong, would be able to deride a non-cricketer in such a manner and get away without a mocking rebuke.

Not through the 'comments' column of an online article or an angry letter to the editor via email, but responded to directly. To the face, so to speak.

It is not athletic progress alone that can be measured in Olympic cycles. An online era means that public responses towards our athletes can also be gauged in that time. During the 2016 Rio Olympics, the reaction to an off-the-cuff remark by a society columnist—'Goal of Team India at the Olympics: Rio jao. Selfies lo. Khaali haat wapas aao. What a waste of money and opportunity[7] (Go to Rio. Take selfies. Return empty-handed.)'—was proof. That an old, tired narrative drummed out often by sports' own governors to reporters could work no more.

~

The generation of athletes that grew up in post-liberalization India was set to become the first of so many things—in the top thirty in singles rankings on the WTA Tour, on the Formula One grid, on the professional squash circuit, on the PGA Tour, Asian medallists in gymnastics, multiple swimming medal winners. As their careers progressed into the twenty-first century, it was the Internet and social media which ensured that the wider public knew how to reach these pioneers directly and follow their careers.

The onset of online/digital journalism, whether through formal websites, blogs or e-papers, meant that Indian sport could now be covered through forms and language unrestricted by space or time, stereotype or bias. It was how the story of sprinter Dutee Chand, forced to undergo a gender test and then banned from competing due to high testosterone levels in her body, could be told with rigour and sensitivity.

Dutee's career was not allowed to go the way of 2006 Doha Asian Games gold medallist Pinki Pramanik, or Santhi Soundarajan, who was stripped of her Doha silver medal over issues of gender identity. In 2006, Pinki and Santhi had been treated as outcasts.

In 2014, after Dutee was dropped from the CWG contingent for Glasgow, there were several factors that ensured her career didn't end abruptly like Pinki's or Santhi's—there was support from the government, a Canadian team willing to fight her case at the Court of Arbitration for Sport, and a journalistic community who wanted to chase the case down to its most minute details. Dutee was given the oxygen she needed to continue her fight, and the fight she needed to be able to run again. The regulations were frozen, Dutee competed at the Rio Olympics, and under the revised athletics regulations, continues to be eligible to race. She is a girl from a family of weavers in Odisha. Not so long ago, she could have been another Pinki or Santhi. The balance of power between Indian athletes and officials has not changed, but the athlete today can be both seen and heard.

The prime agents of change in India across the last decade go beyond merely more proactive government intervention, corporate social responsibility (CSR) tax breaks, the media, or the growth of the Internet. The catalysts in this decade of reinvention happen to be Indian sports' new stakeholders, the unique non-profit intermediaries who have stepped in to do what the official sports federations had shown little interest in doing post-liberalization. Organizations such as the Olympic Gold Quest (formed 2002), Mittal Champions Trust (2003, now defunct), GoSports Foundation (2008), Anglian Medal Hunt (2012) and JSW Sports (2013) are bridge-builders between the aspirational athlete, their federations and funding or expertise. These organizations have also been able to add more towards the media's understanding of what it takes to be a champion. That it is not about those familiar tropes used to explain the failings of Indian athletes across Olympic sports: vegetarianism, lack of killer instinct, genes, lack of ambition or too much love for government jobs. It is not as complicated as we were told earlier. Planning, intention and expertise—get that right and it's as simple as pie.

The specialization of these organizations may be focused on talent identification, individual coaching, logistics and medical treatment/rehabilitation, but their role in bringing attention to their athletes' unique abilities and achievements has added more richness to the narrative around Indian sport. With professional advice, and Twitter and Instagram at hand, athletes can now control their own stories. He said, she said, they said, and things moved.

Although Twitter was founded in 2006, Indian sport and its stars and fans began to take to the news and social networking service starting around 2009–10. Social media broke through the single line of communication between the athlete and conventional media and became an informal, direct, authentic space to chat, which both the athlete and the fan wanted. Twitter became an easy-to-use, no-cost news and PR agency for every athlete, setting up interactions with fans where questions could be asked, announcements made and, if required, controversies stirred—in audio, video or text. Who needed the media?

The stories put out by the athlete would now be their own—no mediator, coach, manager or official speaking for them. Tennis player Sania Mirza is the most followed Indian athlete (8.8 million) outside cricketers on Twitter, and was one of the most prominent early users of the network amongst Indian sportspersons, joining in November 2009. Mahesh Bhupathi (July 2009, 1 million followers) and Narain Karthikeyan (September 2009, 617k followers) had started earlier, and Abhinav Bindra (December 2009, 478k followers) joined a month later.

Sania has been visible and vocal on Twitter, dismissing trolls who attack her for marrying Pakistani cricketer Shoaib Malik, and like the T-shirts that made her famous, speaking her mind. For journalists scrambling to keep pace, social media began to provide its own storylines, quotes and photos. Footballer C.K. Vineeth (July 2014, 179k followers) brought a new level of activism to his social media presence. In January 2018, he posted a photograph of himself along with his friend and fellow footballer Rino Anto with arms locked to express solidarity with a young man who had sat outside the Kerala secretariat in protest over the death of his brother in police custody. In April 2018, following two cases of rapes against minor girls, one of whom was murdered, Vineeth addressed a letter on Twitter to: 'the Prime Minister, Opposition leader, chief justice and every citizen of this country'.[8] In a country where athletes tend to be subservient to politicians of all kinds, at a time where dissent or opposition to the government is being deemed 'anti-national', Vineeth found a way to lodge his protest. At one point during that month, along with Vineeth and Anto again, Sania Mirza, Gautam Gambhir, Sunil Chhetri, Jeev Milkha Singh, Mithali Raj, R. Ashwin, M.C. Mary Kom and Saina Nehwal also expressed their anger on their Twitter handles about the crimes against the minor girls. A decade ago, this would have been impossible to do without holding a press conference.

In June 2018, India football captain Sunil Chhetri (October 2012, 1.5 million followers) did the work of an entire Indian football marketing department by posting a video on his Twitter handle. Disappointed that India's 5-0 victory over Chinese Taipei at the Intercontinental Cup had been before a measly crowd, on 2 June, Chhetri asked the audience, both fans and non-fans—'everyone who is not a football fan [. . .] who have lost hope or do not have any hope in Indian football'—to come watch the team live, rather than 'criticizing them on the Internet'. Chhetri's video said, 'Come to the stadium, scream at us, shout at us, abuse us—who knows one day we might change you guys, you might start cheering for us . . . this is a very important time in Indian football.'[9] The video got more than a million views. The following day, when India played Kenya, the Mumbai Football Arena, small though it may be, was packed. It was Chhetri's hundredth game for India and he scored two goals in the 3-0 win. Circumventing his way past many mediums, the athlete had reached out to the fans, and they had responded with their feet in Mumbai, and around the country, with heartfelt appreciation of Chhetri and his ability to move thousands.

During this decade, Indian sports fans have also reached out in other ways. In October 2009, a Twitter feed under the handle India@Sports was set up by a twenty-seven-year-old, Chandigarh-based sports fan Ravdeep Singh Mehta. To this day, Ravdeep, an independent HR consultant, posts updates on the activity of every Indian athlete across any discipline that he is able to track around the world. His Twitter handle has changed from India@Sports to @India_AllSports, which is described as 'Ultimate Destination for all latest Indian Sports updates (since 2009)',[10] with 23.7k followers. It took nearly six more years for India's sports ministry set up its own official Twitter handle @IndiaSports.[11] At the other end of the scale, a website called 'Nation of Sport' (https://www.nationofsport.com/) was launched in July 2016, to promote long-form writing on Indian sport. It was self-funded by a sports professional, Jonathan Rego, and an ad film director David Rajan, both men in their thirties, and covers the entire gamut of Indian sports—basketball, cricket, football, hockey, Ultimate Frisbee, kabaddi, taekwondo, even fantasy leagues.[12] Nothing is so profane as not to be written about, nothing is too sacred to be inspected closely.

This is an environment so far removed from what Indian sport was like when I began my career, that tales from the 1990s sound like the retelling of a spooky past life. As when Dr Vece Paes of Calcutta (today's Kolkata), father of teenage tennis player Leander, printed out a brochure talking about his son's exploits, talents and promise. The brochure, he said, was to go out to companies asking for sponsorship to somehow finance his son's mission of playing on the professional tennis tour. *This is my boy, this is what he has done, this is what he can do, would you like to support him? With some cash? Please?* To my twenty-something mind, the entire exercise was, in a single breath, both heartbreaking and hard-nosed. What the doctor's sixteen-year-old son did, unashamedly, which made him quite singular, was take pride in waving and owning the Indian flag as if it were his second skin. This was at a time when most Indians were a bit abashed about flaunting their national identity so brazenly. Besides, it wasn't too easy to either buy or fly national flags in the first place. It was like the sixteen-year-old from Calcutta had tapped into a soundtrack that belonged to the future.

Three decades on, every Indian athlete will always be draped in the flag. There is one pasted on to almost every athlete's Twitter handle, with the descriptor 'proud Indian'. The flag finds its way into their speeches, post victory or defeat. The Indian athlete has now emerged as the uber-patriot, the quasi-soldier. And soldiers cannot be doubted or questioned. Which, of course, more than ever, requires that they must always be.

It is a heady time to be listening to or telling stories about Indian sports because of its tumult and volume of activity. There are so many on their search for excellence, wanting to own their slice of history. As Indian sports grows and changes, this is a moment in its sporting history that calls for a more measured recounting. As witnesses and storytellers, we must once again recalibrate our lenses and re-examine our notions.

A wild lover of basketball and rugby after cricket's match-fixing scandal erased all traces of cricket passion in her life, Shivani Naik settled for the disciplined, organized world of Olympic sports, reporting on it for a living. She started writing sport at the *New Indian Express* in Chennai in 2003, covering myriad disciplines like volleyball, fencing, carom, squash and proceeded to mainstream sports like track and field, badminton, tennis and gymnastics, easing into the Olympic lane since moving to Mumbai at the *Indian Express* in 2005. Incurably curious about the everyday eccentricities of sportspersons and attempting to understand their lives, including the perfection of what their limbs and torso execute, Shivani is not terribly impatient while recording the tiny steps Indian sport takes towards its targeted goals of all-round success. She considers herself lucky to be penning stories in an era when the pursuit of an Olympic medal isn't a mechanical step by assembly lines of athletes like in China or America, but a tale of patient fortitude and individual enterprise, as the country figures out its own path to realize its potential.

5

India's March towards Becoming a Multisport Nation

Shivani Naik

They call it the chrysalis stage of a butterfly's metamorphosis. It's that point in time when a dazzling future is imminent, but the takeoff still moments away. A lot may be happening inside the silken shell, even though the world sees quiescence. Countries—even mammoth ones like India—live through these epochs of silent surge. Think back to how cosmonaut Rakesh Sharma trained himself to sit still in spacecraft simulations so that the high accelerations wouldn't cause a weight shift, before he made history as the first Indian in space. Peer back into the time when Avtar Singh Cheema finally ascended the SE Ridge of the Everest after bad weather had packed him and his men off twice—700 and 400 agonizing metres from the pinnacle.

These path-breaking feats, which were culminations of some very inspiring careers, would also be the first tentative steps for the country in their respective precincts. Recall the time when Indians decided to tame and channel the rousing Mahanadi by building the Hirakud dam, or when Goan musicians created the first strains of our jazz music, coming to Bombay every night, playing their saxophones at Alfred's, Marine Lines. Go further back by a century to the time when Sushila Sundari, an accomplished gymnast and trapeze artist in the Great Bengal Circus of the 1890s, brought the crowd to its feet by arm-wrestling with tigers. Or fast-forward to the late 1980s, when the dial-up at IIT Kanpur cost lakhs, so the pioneers of email in India would send emails by courier, writing them on floppies, while still grappling with last-mile connectivity. Those were the giddy days of early development—where the first small steps were taken with a whoop and cheer.

Now think about Indian athletes—and you have the same epoch of sporting chrysalis over the last decade. While the country's glorious hockey past and an ongoing throbbing cricket future bookend the entire narrative of Indian sport, it is in individual sports as varied as shooting, wrestling, boxing, badminton, tennis, gymnastics, rowing and fencing that the country is on the brink of takeoff, as the winds are caught in the gliders. India is nowhere among the top contenders for leading Olympic tables yet; we still audit the Olympics with collective gasping and grunting and grudging over our single-digit frivolous returns every four years. But the last decade and a half has been a time of a cheerful but choppy churn in Indian sport.

These are stories of individual enterprise, tales of lonely journeys fuelled by nothing other than drive and motivation.

These are still minor victories when compared to the world's sporting behemoths—edging the Chinese out in shooting here, and overpowering the might of the erstwhile Soviet in wrestling there. Taking incremental toddler steps in tennis and rowing one moment, and showing the audacity to stamp grace and grit in badminton on the rest of the world the very next. Going past just throwing darts in the dark in fencing and archery, and storming boxing rings to land a charismatic knockout punch. The last decade has seen India bound out of its self-limiting confines and burst out like the rays of the sun.

But in zooming in on the precise moments of triumph of these outliers, we gaze into the last muscle sinew of their bodies and pore over the streams of thought that zipped through their minds. In joining these dots, we record India's tiny blinks on the global sports radar. But as our man in space noted, it all started with learning to sit still while the world of G-forces swirled around. In sport, Abhinav Bindra, India's only individual gold medallist, started this folklore by standing regally still amidst what was typically Indian chaos.

It's a record in Indian *shooting* as boast-worthy as the Indian cricket team's World Cup stat against Pakistan. Except, India's four shooting medallists won't boast that they all left a Chinese in their wake: Bindra blazed past a wailing Zhu Qinan for a gold, double trap shooter R.V.S. Rathore quelled back a chasing pack with Zheng Wang nudged to a bronze, silver medallist Vijay Kumar shrugged off Ding Feng who sat back at third place, and Gagan Narang denied Tao Wang a medal altogether, pinning him to fourth. Quite simply, no Indian shooting medallist has allowed a Chinese to overtake him on the medal pave till now.

India's first medal at the London Games, in fact, came in the ghostly silent vacuum Narang created for himself after Tao had already taken the shot that blinked 10.4. The crowd had started one right dinning ruckus as Narang needed a minimum 10.1. (In qualification, he had foozled a pair of 9s around the 53rd shot). But he would shoot a 10 point serene 7, to puncture Chinese hopes in 2012.

Perhaps the most commanding of Chinese put-downs was Abhinav Bindra's charge towards the gold—epochal enough for the host's biggest newspaper to splash him on their front page. Rathore had teed off at Athens with India's first silver. But most of India's bustling teen population in 2008 had never known what it was to win an Olympic gold. When Bindra's came, it was almost imperative that the core of that success be earnest endeavour drizzled with excellence. His precise preparation would later spawn a tome of transcendence. But it was in that downing of the Chinese that the soundless Bindra ballad reached its crescendo. For the man, the high point was him fighting 10.7 right after his sighting shot had caused the greatest turbulence of his life, needing a gun realignment to get back on track. To the world, it was the 10.8—a moment of epic clarity and release for the young man given to self-doubt and constant questioning. Bindra would take his final Beijing shot clearly, quickly, aggressively and courageously. The trigger pulled in those nano-moments between the fourth and the fifth heartbeat of seconds, he was the first person to shoot, and showed just how regal perfection could look. Perfection measured 10.8 that noon in Shijingshan district. Unusually calm the evening before, his coach Gaby had incited a tiny panic attack in Bindra to shake him out of the uncharacteristic tranquillity. His old fiendish companion—the feeling of a stabbing sword in the gut and the chest—had promptly fetched up. But Bindra had rehearsed to deal with even this eventuality, and he slayed it like a boss. The gold was to come at the end of such meticulous preparation that he'd effectively buried India's usual propensity to laid-back preparation which saw athletes turning up on the day and hoping that fate would somehow rule in their favour. He had prepared his body for both the stabbing feeling in the gut and the wavering mind which could lose the plot as it did briefly in his sixth series. It was a 10.9 (out of 10.9) in preparation that yielded the 10.8 on the final shot.

Vijay Kumar also had a 100 per cent to boast. In classes seven and eight, he'd won the only certificates he did in his academic life, for cent per cent attendance at school in Himachal. But going beyond his capacity to work very hard and very diligently, this average student shaped up to become a special pistol shooter from the army. His palm size was larger than average, helping with the pistol grip. His reflexes when the target light blinked from red to green were extraordinary (at its toughest, you fire five shots in four seconds on targets in a straight line). And he could pack it all in—watch the blinking light, lift his hand, align sights, pull the 1-kg trigger lever, soak in the recoil and control the heartbeat—over and over again, shot after shot after shot.

While the recoil of a 7.62 mm sniper's weapon in the army can even dislocate shoulders, single-handed triggering on the 25-metre Rapid Fire pistol range brings its own tremoring of the shoulder that Vijay's time-bound duelling entailed. While Vijay went into the Olympics having done well in the quick-fire format of five targets in 8-6-4 seconds, routinely racking up scores of 585, he was up against World Cup medallists with over twenty-five wins under their belt in the final. It's in the tenacity and work rate of his last six months after winning a quota in 2011 that Vijay literally moulded the pattern that culminated in the silver. Giving up oily, spicy food (a habit he's maintained), training his body physically for two hours, fine-tuning a technique he'd come to trust and eschewing the urge to try anything new at the last moment, Vijay set into force a habit. He had trained his mind to live in the moment, focus only on the input and perish all stray thoughts of outcome. All he felt was the strain of lifting the gun for six to seven hours. He was priming to succeed by not allowing anything to distract him. On Finals day, he did the only thing he knew—stick to a plan, barely caring for scores or standings. A medal eluding him would've surprised him—his silver, he reckons, was the most logical conclusion.

Yet, the spell was broken in 2016, when India returned with no medals in shooting. A shaky tile in the floor or the tremulous pulling of the rug from under the feet, Indian shooters had been known to find steadiness in the storm that is Indian sport. Only the sturdiest hearts learned to imbibe the recoil, and win. All four even edged the Chinese to a notch below India.

The country now awaits its first female Olympic medallist in shooting. Those medals have been China's preserve for some time now—but that's the rite of passage into India's shooting pantheon.

Yet another of India's medal sports saw its prologue scribbled at the 2004 Games. India's washout in two days at Persiteri Hall in Athens was the inception of a decade-long surge in *boxing*. But while it lasted, it was a widely adored sport with two of India's most charismatic athletes—Vijender Singh and M.C. Mary Kom, who won medals. It was in the quick wrap-up in Athens that Brig. Murlidhar Raja, an astute referee and judge from India, hit the eureka moment. Judges those days were under the pump after computerized consoles had been introduced, and only the cleanest of punches were getting marked, since mistakes reflected poorly on judging capabilities. The cleanest punches were the straightest punches, and word was sent out by Brig. Raja right down to sub-junior and junior ranks that the low-yielding hooks and uppercuts were to be refrained from.

The one man who bought into this unreservedly was the one who won India's first Olympic medal in boxing—a bronze at Beijing. There had been quicker and feistier boxers before—the 1960s' heroes right up to Dingko Singh and Mohammed Ali Qamar, who fought on sheer gumption. But Vijender was a smart cookie behind that impish young facade. Intuitive in his movements, always knowing where he ought to be and with sharp punches, Vijender didn't go wading into unnecessary skirmishes and unsolicited bravado that could cost him points. The Mittal Champions Trust had come in looking to help and their

CEO Manisha Malhotra had roped in as performance director the revered physiotherapist Heath Matthews from South Africa who brought in, amongst other things, the ice bath that helped in recovery. Akhil Kumar, a dashing pugilist, would kick-start the headlines, beating Russian world champ Sergey Vodopyanov before being felled tactically by Moldovan Gojan, who struck from behind his shell guard. But it was the unheralded yet meticulous Vijender who would corner the medal. Vijender was economical with his hits but smart in the final ten seconds, imprinting his concisely effective game on the judges' minds. So, while Akhil threw 300 punches, for Vijender, a third of that number sufficed. He didn't rely excessively on speed (for that's the first to ditch the body). For Vijender's technique was sheer timing, almost like the smoothness with which cricketer Inzamam piled up run mountains without apparent violence. An Asian Games gold in 2010 followed after that win over Ecuadorian Carlos Gongora at the Olympics that gave him a bronze.

Mary Kom's many medals and magnificence came from a place of grit, where her mind told her very early that she could beat anyone, never mind the size of the opponent. All of her six World Championships and medals at the Olympics, Asiad and CWG, spanning childbirths (yes, multiple) and injuries, happened because she never stayed content with what she'd achieved. The wolfish appetite for wins awed her opponents as well. Such as Karolina Michalczuk of Poland, taller and bigger, but infinitely more rattled by Mary than Mary was by her. The Indian was a natural at 48 kg, but, forced to fight in 51, she would build up her menace. The trick to enjoying a Mary bout was to watch her feet—if others her size lunged a metre and a half, she always had 6 inches more with added feline speed, with the short punches packing enough power. While light on her feet, she had such a hold over Romanian Duta Stuleta (whom she beat for four of her five world titles) that she seemed to be acing both the dancing shuffle of the cha-cha and the tactical positioning of chess, driving opponents giddy in the same ring. Before London, she was weighing herself six times a day, and while she beat the Polish girl at 50.9, she would go down to Nicola Adams at a slightly weaker 50.2 and return with an Olympic bronze. The revolution didn't quite take off in women's boxing or in Manipur as it ought to have. But this only proved how two immensely driven and talented individuals made it an Indian boxing spring lasting half a dozen years.

It wasn't shooting or boxing, though, that had racked up the buzz heading into the 2008 Games. All talk that year, Satpal 'Pahalwan' remembers, was about how tennis would bring the medal from Beijing. India's tennis doubles stars had recall value coach Satpal Singh knew his wrestlers didn't. *'Medal kya ped pe ugte hai?* (Do you think medals grow on trees?),' he would be asked in the typically Haryanvi trenchant tone when he started talking about a whiff of a *wrestling* medal India had last won in 1952 through Khashaba Jadhav. But Satpal had chanced upon a young boy who did many things right. He had come in as an ordinary 28-kg lad, one of the many from Delhi's outback lands in Haryana, wanting to wrestle for India. But he was rare, in that when asked to do 1000 *baithak*s, he would do 1500. He rarely hid out in the bathrooms when chased to push his body further in crunches. Most importantly, when he grew up, he refused a plum post in the CRPF (Central Reserve Police Force) which would've brought home a big pay cheque but effectively ended his wrestling *taalim*. And so Satpal decided to answer the cackling doubters by planning for Sushil Kumar's first medal.

At Athens, he would miss out in a close bout. At Beijing, though, hungrier and stronger at 66 kg, Sushil would shrug off the early loss and bring home a bronze by repêchage. Bringing wrestling back to India's centre stage had taken a lot of detailed plotting. A month before the Games, Satpal had recced Beijing, arranging for the necessary Indian food for his wrestlers. Everything from documenting the hall temperatures to dossiers on all possible opponents were prepared. Satpal, Sushil and a younger Yogeshwar Dutt would sit till late into the night watching videos of opponents and looking for openings to exploit. The Beijing show would merely loosen drawstrings. The whole bag was prised open, in London. Wrestling typically bunches up towards the end of the Olympics. India had already had its best Games in terms of number of medals (no gold, though) at London, with four, when wrestling began. Yogeshwar had run up a good charge after losing out to the eventual finalist, and this time, all of India knew that repêchage was French for a second shot at the medal, albeit a bronze. What no one knew was just how spectacular a bronze medal play-off could look when Yogeshwar took on North Korean Ri Jong-Myong. In what was a series of leg-twisters, known as the *phitle daanv*,

Yogeshwar would seal a leg hold and flip his opponent repeatedly to get the stadium on its feet and whooping for the audacity and skill of that pristine *akhara* move of the Indian, playing itself out on the global stage of the shiny mat. A day later, Sushil would stomp up to the final with a thundering display of strength and ferocity. The Kazakh Akzhurek Tanatarov was hauled off his feet and flung to the floor, the *bhaarandaaz* takedown in all its gargantuan glory unleashed upon his opponent in the semi-final. He was also accused of 'rudeness'—his teeth drew blood from his opponent's ear—but that nasty business will remain the inconclusive mystery of Indian sport, even as the silver is feted for long. A low-crouching style, a pair of twinkling toes that could win a game of Twister, some feral strength not only in thrashing opponents in the manner of Hulk-getting-annoyed-with-Loki but also a strangulating strength that could puncture rival bodies, and finally a pick of 500 daanvs to choose from at any given moment: Sushil had all that, and cleverness that has helped him in battles—on and off the mat. A gold eluded him, but that miss has kept him hungry, pushing his career for half a dozen years more as he attempts a medal in the 74 kg now.

Strength was in no shortage for Sakshi Malik too. Things had looked grim till the thirteenth day of the Rio Olympics, when the then twenty-two-year-old from Rohtak effected her trademark 'double leg' move—a series of ramming actions that end in a takedown executed at lightning speed, to bring India its first medal of the Games. Sakshi was a silver medallist from CWG and a bronze finisher at the Asian, and was largely unheralded going into the Olympics, qualifying in only the last of cut-off events. But what she had was silent determination to make the most of coming from oblivion, and blindsiding opponents in the most crucial moments. The double leg was a signature statement of immense strength—she summoned it in each of her five bouts at Rio. But more importantly, Malik had the ability to fly under the radar for the longest time and capture the moment when it was time. Not all ambitions are grandly articulated or need elegiac epilogues. Sakshi's medal was path-breaking because she became India's first woman wrestler to step up on the podium, of course, but if sporting success was about grabbing the moment by its throat and making it count forever, Sakshi had mastery over the leg double—to execute it at the right time, to smother all resistance for a pin-down, to have the utter ballsy confidence to watch the clock ticking out and still keep an even heart rate till seconds before she launched a breathtaking counter. History was pinned down.

Not all history, though, is a manic twisting of limbs and a moment's power play. Some success in sport is like a slow-cooking, flavoursome stew. *Badminton*, for instance. If sporting excellence is about turning up day after day, battling a new opponent and newer challenge across the net every morning you wake up, and finishing as the last woman standing, Saina Nehwal will beat every other sportsperson from India hands down. Ten Superseries titles, ten Grand Prix crowns, two Commonwealth Games individual golds, a clutch of team-leading, bronze medal podium finishes at CWG, Uber Cup and Asian Games, two World Championship medals—a silver and a bronze and, of course, Indian badminton's first Olympic medal—a bronze at London: a breathless list of honours, each of which came on the back of a week of frenzied focus packed meticulously into a filed folder of triumph. Not just one day of brilliance. Not simply a dash of sub-10 seconds of momentous exhilaration. Not merely one decisive move that cornered spectacular glory, but at least twenty-six weeks of solid, steely discipline in painstakingly welding, crafting and tuning up to win all those above-mentioned medals.

They used to say Indians didn't quite have the 'body'— the fast-twitch fibres, the calf muscles, the ripped core— to lord over in badminton. So Saina Nehwal went out there and strung together a body of work. Some lifetimes get crunched into that one grand moment when the amalgamated effort comes together to deliver coveted success, but Nehwal filled every corner of the page with her tweaks, her invisible hours spent perfecting one stroke, her travails and her travels while stamping her class on the hallowed arenas of badminton across China, Indonesia and Europe. It was evident in 2006, when she lost the gold to Chinese Yihan Wang at the World Juniors in Korea and when she stepped up to help India win the bronze at the Commonwealth Games in Melbourne, that this was going to be a gladiatorial fighter who will win a lot. But when not, she'd not go down without a battle. She started out with a whiplash smash and not much more in her arsenal. She wasn't the most sprightly of presences on the court, nor someone with a wrist that could weave intricate webs of deception. But the last ten years have seen Nehwal painstakingly nuance the big kill by learning the half-smash, getting a commanding grip on net play, working on her striding movements to compensate for the lack of natural agility and outlasting all her contemporaries to always remain in contention.

For the longest time in her early days of success, she went without injuring herself, and when the knee did cave in, Nehwal had the resilience to return well enough to win another World Championship medal. While the once World No. 1's game has adapted to the passage of time, what will remain an enduring image of Saina Nehwal is her unbreakable grit and mental strength—she, like Mary, first believed she could beat anyone in the world, and in her second avatar, she has proven she has the fortitude to carve out title wins for herself, never mind how much the wear and tear has nibbled at her core. She might never start as a championship-favourite ever, given the surfeit of talent in women's singles globally, but no one can rule out Saina Nehwal in any contest she enters.

India's greatest moment in badminton, though, came at the Rio Olympics, when P.V. Sindhu brought into full imposing glory the might of her height while making a charge at the Olympics final in the 2016 Games. A tad more talented than Nehwal, Sindhu had more than just the flapping range of her arms. A more expansive range of strokes, savage power and hand-speed when in peak shape, she was no mug at deception when she strung together wins against some of the game's biggest names in her dash to the Rio finals. Playing one of the most enthralling finals against Carolina Marin, Sindhu came pretty close to the biggest prize there is in the game. Of course, the near-six-footer had first come to notice with a pair of World Championship bronze medals—mopping up the whole might of the Chinese at the annual big event. She could scythe through entire draws, chomping on the top Chinese names, though she hit the next gear post her silver at Rio. It has been in her recent battles against the Japanese—some of the most consummate practitioners currently—and her ability to battle in titanic marathons throughout 2017, that Sindhu has added the most important dimension to badminton viewing in India. She's been part of three of the most-watched women's singles finals through the last two years—Olympics '16, Worlds '17 and Superseries Finals '17. Not only has she got the partisans to root for her, but she has also managed to catapult women's singles into being the most thrilling event in the sport, shading the men's game, which still boasts two of the all-time greats. Between them, and while separately hiking the ascent to the apex, Saina Nehwal and P.V. Sindhu have pursued excellence in unconventional ways—carrying the swag and grace of physical and mental strength.

But the legacy of India's traditional deft touch—all pretty strokes and wristwork, all the smoothness and plenty of time on the shuttle—is carried forward by Kidambi Srikanth, a winner of six Superseries titles. Perhaps winning coach Pullela Gopichand's biggest challenge yet, Srikanth, who reached the World No. 1 position last year (the first to do so after Prakash Padukone), has many boxes to tick in terms of medals at the Olympics and World Championships. He also has the likes of H.S. Prannoy (a masterful backhand shuttler) and the skilful B. Sai Praneeth flanking him as India moves forward with throbbing pace in the men's singles.

The likes of Jwala Gutta, V. Diju and Ashwini Ponnappa sought and found success in doubles over the last decade, with medals at CWG and the Worlds. But it is down to the young pairing of Satwiksairaj Rankireddy and Chirag Shetty to truly break ground on the circuit and complete India's set, which has sorely lacked in world-class achievement in the men's doubles. It will take Saina's belief and Sindhu's raw spirit to garner the sort of consistent headlines in doubles that the singles command now.

In another racquet sport shaded most noticeably by badminton, Sania Mirza's doubles headlines would wind up bloating more than her short singles spell. But India had gotten caught up in the maudlin maze of doubles success by then, and Sania Mirza's briefest of dazzles in *tennis* faded out. It's not as if it was tough to stay focused on Mirza's forehand. But India revels in its silly distractions and Mirza's story was mired in it all—what she wore, what she said, where the tricolour was when she sat in the stands, whom she married and whose side she was on in the almighty whirlpool of Indian tennis—the great anti-love story of its doubles couple. But amidst India's doubles flare-ups, which were as passive-aggressive as an Icelandic volcano, there once flew the Sania Mirza forehand. If hitting groundstrokes was all there was to tennis, Mirza would've debuted in the Top Ten and stayed there awhile. The forehand was especially world-class at a time when Indian women traded in moon-balls and their versions of the occasional canny volley. Mirza struck it flat, and could direct it from anywhere on the court for a winner. Wins against Kuznetsova, Zvonareva, Bartoli, Hingis, Safina and Azarenka came in the heady days when she peaked at World No. 27. But a limited serve and fitness troubles meant she toppled out of the singles orbit after a few years. Her Plan B took years to form and execute, and did enable her to enjoy the view from the top of the world in women's doubles for a nice, long while. But the world soon figured out that if you made her run hard, you could blunt the swag in her shot. Still, for both how spectacularly the comet took off and how furiously fast it faded out, Sania Mirza's was easily the most dazzling spectacle of the last decade. It was a risky game, especially on the women's tour, where safe strokes and dull but durable solid defence prevailed. When it got going, Sania Mirza reached dizzying heights, but when she started missing, there were no safety nets. And India returned intermittently to its doubles feuds.

Nothing, however, exemplified India's sporting diversity better than the emergence of another bolt of lightning talent—*archer* Deepika Kumari from a village on Ranchi's outskirts. Big medals on mammoth stages— the Olympics singularly—tend to be the parameter for judging peak achievement, though, like Sania, this live wire can't boast the big medal. Deepika remarkably failed on that stage in both London and Rio. But for the sheer journey she made, coming from utter poverty and the absolute hinterland to achieving the World No. 1 ranking (2012) and equalling the world record score of 686/720, the twenty-four-year-old will remain Indian sport's most dazzling shooting star. The country has lost count of the number of times Deepika has crumbled in crunch-duels, that one-on-one contest that caters to a spectator's need for contrasting the great with the non-great. Left to herself with a recurve bow and a modern quiver of arrows—just girl versus her goal—Deepika can appear almost regal when shooting.

But medals are won in cruel coliseums, drowning the din and the decibel, downing the constraints and the criticism. In that, the enigma of the woman has let down, and not without a bitter scowl and some thwarting anger. Indian archery exists on treacherous quicksand: the year-round selection trials inexplicably test endurance and not the one-on-one duels—so archers are hardly buffed up to soak up that pressure. Foreign coaches—necessary but not neat fits—tend to be Koreans with plenty of trouble for archers who come from remote areas and don't speak the same tongue. The federation remains cloistered in its benighted ideas of what constitutes Olympic-level training. A mental trainer could sort things out a little to draw Deepika out of the defensive shell she's wrapped around herself, but all of it has never come together. Stung by early failures and scarred by the harsh spotlight, Deepika Kumari hurtles from one big competition to the next, tripping at the same points over and over again, staying content with those scattered medals at World Cups. She may well be overtaken someday by an archer not so tormented by expectations. But if she can fight back from the corner she seems to be perennially stuck in, the archer can be one of the most dramatic stories of Indian sport.

Nevertheless, even the smallest flickers of light can race through the grim desolation that used to be Indian sport a decade ago, when athletes were still diffident. Ashish Kumar had spent his first Commonwealth Games clicking shy pictures with India's medal-minting shooters at Melbourne in 2006. Four years on, in Delhi, he wanted to be front and centre in those podium-winning pictures in *gymnastics*. But in the gold glut at the Karni Singh shooting range of the 2010 Games, a bronze at the Indira Gandhi Arena in Gymnastics' Floor Exercise and a sensational silver on the Vaulting table (India's first in gymnastics) were a tad lost in the celebratory cacophony. But it was the solitary bronze a month later at the Guangzhou Asian Games that was like the Rube Goldberg machine set rolling by two Indians— first Ashish and later, Dipa Karmakar. India was still years away from acing the consistency drill of mainstream moves in gymnastics—the ones that the pros perfected after countless repetition. Indians needed a spectacular contraption that could yield the big points, but after what would be a severely complicated and at times convoluted course. What Ashish would do over that October– November Asiad of 2010 would start this domino drive—a set of complex moves imbibed to hit the high Difficulty-scores, going for broke. While the then nineteen-year-old had kicked off the trend with high D-scores of 6.500 (next best was a gold-winning 6.100) on Floor and 7.000 on the Vault in Delhi, Ashish would enter the dragon's domain in China. In what would be one of the biggest upsets of that year, the Indian would pip China's world champion on the Parallel Bars, Zhe Feng, to the bronze. This was done with his first line of routine which boasted something that no one in the world was risking that year—a round, off-back, 900-degree twist to forward double *salto*.

The challenge was in combining two sets of movements that were completely opposing to each other in momentum (cartwheels going back that merged seamlessly into somersaults going forward in one smooth motion). This needed very good judgement of knowing when to finish the first line and connect it to the reverse one mid-air—a dizzying acrobatic feat that the gymnast had improvised during training and shown the guts to unveil in the international spotlight. It was a 6.300 routine—not the highest score—and he had two Chinese, a pair of Koreans and Japanese, and an Uzbeki going for the podium in the final. But then there was his uniquely bold first line: a back salto, powered front double followed by a series—two twisting somersaults, then a backflip that had him turn in the air thrice. A jerk-free, smooth dismount completed the routine, though it was the opening line that had catapulted Ashish into Asia's Top 3. It was like Ritchie Blackmore's classic riff in 'Smoke on the Water'—a four-note hat tip to Beethoven—only with the Indian plucking the right chords with his own contortionist's body. Ashish had dug deep into his sixteen years of training starting with tumbles and handstands at the age of four in Allahabad, and mined out an opening that was rare and rewarding, surprising the military drill-like Asian field.

Four seasons later, Dipa Karmakar aced this peculiar Indian penchant for fearlessness, attempting the outrageous. There's beauty in bold stomping of the runway and taking off like a plane with limbs for wings. Dipa had the speed in her legs and power in her core to pull off the Produnova—a front handspring, double salto—for what was called the 'vault of death'. It was demanding and dangerous, with very few in the world going for broke. It could assure a high starting D-score, but pulling it off to its logical conclusion without seriously harming oneself was the devil's rider. Dipa, driven by the scorching urge to win the medal she reckoned she'd missed in 2010, importantly had the courage and discipline to follow through on that adrenaline surge. Guided by coach Bisweswar Nandi, this Tripura girl would dream and dare and do what was required. Success wasn't a one-off, though the big medal came at Glasgow's Commonwealth Games in 2014, a bronze after just fifty-odd repetitions. But she would repeat the Produnova over and over again—in unglamorous, unspectacular surroundings, with her coach and co-trainees watching—to prep for the Olympics.

A foam pit was her safety net, but while the Russian Yelena Produnova had debuted this vault, which the men routinely performed as the 'Roche', Dipa Karmakar's rendition of the Produnova at the CWG, the Asiad and the Worlds as well as the Olympics thereafter, brought it an almost prosaic efficacy. Not that the risk was somehow reduced. Just that Dipa tamed the set of actions to such a proficient extent that the world got accustomed to watching her with admiration rather than the customary dread. Dipa would light up the Rio Games for India, and with yet another seamless execution, go right up to fourth in the standings. The medal wasn't won, but the Indian was the toast of the world for maintaining the sanctity of the sport—staying safe even while pulling off one of the world's most difficult acrobatic feats, performed by a strong, beautiful woman. They got used to believing: it was an Indian.

Around the same timelines, another set of Indians—very unlike the gymnasts in their body-type—were hurling, not themselves, but objects sacred to the world of athletics in the world of *throws*. The lite heavies of athletics—discus and javelin throwers (as against hammer and shot-putters where the beefy European heavy heavies swarm)—have been the breakthrough story in India's track and field sports of the last decade. For far too long, the millisecond misses and fourth places of the many illustrious runners Milkha Singh, Sriram Singh and P.T. Usha have run the reels of nostalgia rather than the actual number of medals. The pining for the athletic medal is so drenched in those heroic disappointments that the country has taken its time to notice the vast expanse of the green field in the middle of the red track, around which tiring eyes have followed the tragic tales of these runners even as the hurlers have come into their own. But then came the Commonwealth Games in Delhi, where Krishna Poonia led a 1-2-3 charge in the discus throw to a rousing roar of the home fans. At her peak, Krishna followed the pertinacious path of consistency—always at 63 metres or thereabouts, which would put her in the Top 7 of any competition. It was this unfailing ability to put herself into contention that ensured that when the stars aligned—a depleted field at CWG and a dreamy starlit night at the Jawaharlal Nehru Stadium—Krishna's 61.51 metres helped her lead the podium charge.

There was a silver for India in that Games as well, which would balloon into a grand gold—India's finest (and tallest at 6 ft 9 in.)—at the CWG four years later in Glasgow. It was the big man Vikas Gowda, with his windmill arms and the giant frame that could accrue angular acceleration and detonating release for a 63.64 throw to reward one of India's most resilient athletes. Labouring through Maryland and Arizona in the USA, and with only his father holding steady that torquing spine when confronted with official apathy, the Mysuru thrower who also taught math at a school to supplement his earnings, would end up being India's most consistent performer at the Olympics.

What's pushed the bar—rather, a spear—further is the precocious talent of Neeraj Chopra. A youth world champion who was credited with having natural nous for the arrowing technique of the 800-gram javelin, Chopra learnt his craft watching YouTube videos and 3D-printing the finest actions into his limbs and torso. It would need an inherent intelligence to break down that movement of building linear speed and sending it upwards of 80 metres, and Chopra triggered a generational jump in the distances Indians were propelling. Suddenly there is now a clutch of juniors dreaming of the spear soaring beyond 75 metres. Of course, Chopra—who has now progressed from learning from seniors and the Web to some of the best coaches in the world—would need to breach that psychological barrier of 90 metres—with a bunch of Germans piercing it. Hitting that mark in the run-up to Tokyo could well put India in that orbit of realistic expectation in a discipline that's never fetched a medal. Chopra's always had a kinesiological hunch on the technique to transfer energy and hurl the javelin farthest. But even better, he might've jacked up the aspirations of many others in India.

Attempting another impossibility and treading completely uncharted territory like the throwers, are the *rowers*. The gastrocnemius and soleus muscles, and the quadriceps are what every rower ought to be obsessed with. The Europeans, the Americans, the Kiwi world-beater Mahe Drysdale, and even the new-age Chinese push off the oars with the power emanating from flexing these lower-leg muscular lobes. In India, though, rowers keep one wary eye on the Salmonella. The typhoid-causing bacteria have proven to be a scourge for India's top rowers, felling them ahead of competitions—though India's graph in single sculls has kept getting better at each one of the last three Olympics despite these setbacks. And to think that India's army rowers confront the most pitiful conditions imaginable: no water, and worse, dirty waters.

Bajrang Lal Takhar rowed single sculls in Beijing. He came from Sikar, in dry, arid Rajasthan. One of the palace lakes had hosted India's first Nationals, but the luxury of synchronizing strokes on a streamlined boat wasn't something Bajrang grew up with. Ahead of the 2012 Games, he went down due to typhoid and his career packed up.

Swarn Singh Virk, whose high point came in Eton during the London Games, with him finishing in the Top 16, also had the most rotten strokes of luck with his career. He comes from Mansa, a polluted village in Punjab, notorious for its floating industrial effluents. When he took up rowing in Hyderabad after joining the army, a back injury and some serious motivation issues later, Swarn was yanked back again by typhoid ahead of the Asiad in 2018.

For India's reigning champ, Dattu Bhokanal, coming off a bold Rio Games showing, his rowing started at Evla Taluka in Nashik—he'd seen his fair share of drought and drinking-water shortages. Still water was still a novelty for him, as clean water was for Swarn after years of training in Hyderabad at Hussain Sagar Lake, with its thick sludge of garbage from Kukatpally nala. It's tragically revealing that these challenges can prove debilitating even before the ergometer (the rowing simulator) throws up its row-specific numbers and lung-capacity max figures. That India still competes for the single sculls gold—no less—at the Asiad is more a statement about the army men's efforts to literally stay afloat.

The youngest of these trendsetters in terms of the number of years taken for the sport to incubate, though, has been another sharp blade, but of a different kind. You can never tell what catches a girl's fancy. In Bhavani Devi's case, it was the white mask, the jacket, the sword and the electronic equipment in *fencing*. She was good at math in school, but precision was more fun when the blitzing thrust of the sabre set off a light. She always had quick reflexes. In India, the best fencers came from Manipur, while Punjab and Kerala girls were no mugs with the blunted blades. But Bhavani, from Chennai, was just that much more discreet and calculated in her lunges to emerge as one of India's first international contenders in fencing. Eight years after starting out with a junior team bronze in the Asian Cadet championship in 2009, Bhavani would claim her first gold in 2017. Training in Italy currently, where fencing is more mainstream than in Asia, she's learning from the European masters, while ensuring that they get accustomed to having a highly motivated Indian in their midst. Always decisive since her childhood and knowing exactly what she wanted to do in life, this Chennai girl has opened a novel flank for Indians in a sport that might seem foreign but is severely suited to the Indian work ethic and the general tendency to stay doggedly dedicated.

While the sabre sets a lot of store by speed, it is in the economy of using that slashing pace—knowing when to and when not to—that winners get decided. Bhavani has just the right amount of smarts to open up new vistas for Indians in the coming years. The Koreans and the Chinese, though, rule this event at the world level, and it'll be a patient wait before India watches the sword scythe through all the competition. While her emotional energy and physical power are all channelled into finding success in fencing, it is in the technique and its nous that the Indian will have to take giant strides. As it happens in fencing, it could well be two steps forward, one step back. For the sheer audacity to think she could ace a sport as alien in excellence to India as fencing, and for venturing out—first to Kerala SAI from Chennai, and then all the way to Italy for longer stints—Bhavani and her modest family that adores its daughter deserve all the props.

In one of India's easternmost corners, another young girl, also twenty-two, has traversed a long journey of her own in *weightlifting*. Failures are the best fuel for future success.

And there was one Indian who could stack them disappointments all on to barbells—yellow, red and green— and defy gravity with such precise gnashing geometry that Mirabai Chanu would become the country's Hercules in November 2017 with an imperious weightlifting World Championship title. A year earlier at Rio, she had crumpled into a nervous heap on the big stage, unable to bring India another weightlifting Olympic medal—sixteen years after Karnam Malleswari, India's first woman medallist. Mirabai, from Manipur, is prodigiously talented—her muscle quality, her intuitive body balance that can shoulder four times her body weight, and finally her indestructible love for the sport, which bloomed when she joined the rest of India in idolizing yesteryears lifter Kunjarani Devi.

The Olympic disappointment tested her severely, but she emerged like a shining metal disc from the foundry, forged from bubbling resolve. At the World's in Anaheim in the next season, Mirabai would gather memories of all her previous setbacks (those that crumbled in the spotlight and those faced alone in the darkest corners of her mind), and heave an almighty 196 kg for a world-class gold, two decades after Malleswari. It needed plenty of technique tweaks from her professorial coach Vijay Sharma, who has studied the sport in such minute detail that he could meticulously put together all the body physiology and boulder physics to correct Mirabai's flaws step by step, and lift her out of the depression she had gone through after the Rio Games.

When on a roll, Mirabai looks nothing less than the snatch-clean-and-jerk variant of the lion-skin-wearing

Roman God who could lift the sky. But the 2016 miss has rooted her so tight to the ground that only the Tokyo medal will put her at ease. Mirabai, though, is ensuring that women's sport's grandest legacy in weightlifting is carried forward—rather, hoisted high— with her explosive power all scrunched into those crucial moments when a mere 5-ft tall woman summons all her will to lift upwards of 100 kg—her body aligned through taut sinews for a spectacular show of power.

No less a Herculean effort belonged to a young man who had had his arm amputated after touching a live wire when climbing a tree as a child. From there to two gold medals at the highest sporting stage, was *paralympian* Devendra Jhajharia's Iliad. The *kotinos*—those olive wreaths that crowned medallists' heads—were just the same. The way fellow athlete Deepa Malik remembers Athens, the way R.V.S. Rathore slung a Perazzi around his shoulder like a cool cat and the manner in which the wreath sat regally on Devendra Jhajharia's head were identical, right down to the steely glint of intent in their eyes when they went about the business of winning medals.

Even 56-kg powerlifter Rajinder Singh Rahelu donned that iconic wreath with Jhajharia, an F 44/46-category, javelin-throwing champion at the Athens Paralympics. Except, India didn't quite put on the pedestal in the same way the two wreaths that were exactly the same as the one that defined shooting's successful Olympic debut.

Malik reckons that the overwhelming adoration in 2016 when India's four Paralympic medals got feted the same way as its two at the able-bodied Games finally made her rewrite the dull, heartbreaking pain she'd felt about those two ignored wreaths from a dozen years ago.

The turning point of the Paralympics movement in the country was Jhajharia's 2004 gold. That Malik would claim her own place in history as India's first woman Para medallist alongside Jhajharia, who sensationally returned in 2016 to reclaim his gold with a world-record-breaking throw, just made the Rio Games a seminal moment in India's sporting history. High jumper Mariyappan Thangavelu added to the joy with his gold.

Besides the two golds and Malik's silver, Varun Bhati would add another bronze to the high jump, bringing the all-time Indian Paralympic medal tally up to twelve (four glittering golds, four shimmering silvers and four bold bronze medals). Each carried a story of extreme fortitude unimaginable to their able-bodied counterparts, or to the clueless citizenry.

While the earlier Paralympians had been completely weaned off support or empathy (1972 gold medallist Murlikant Petkar only won the Padma Shri in 2018) with ignorance prevailing, the Paralympic athletes of today remain miles behind their counterparts from other countries in sports science. While most developed countries have advanced rapidly in both physiotherapy for the disabled and technological backup, India has only just woken up to the disability cause. A country that is still fighting for ramps at public places—the most rudimentary of necessities—has clearly not warmed up to the scientific challenge of kitting out its Para athletes on the sports field with techno aids to get better at sport, or even to ease their daily life.

Jhajharia, Malik and Mariyappan were clearly driven by motivation that they had mined deep down from their own core. While the lanky Rajasthani had been told by his mother after his hand needed an amputation that he ought to go out and play and not stay cooped up indoors, it was the restless love for the outdoors that pushed Malik to take up Para athletics when she was paralysed at the brink of thirty.

Her first diagnosis of tumour as a child had left her fervently pining for a chance to play with children as she watched them from the window. So, when her health was restored, she had taken to adventure and sport with passion, her love for bikes paralleled only by her wish to do well on the field. Both she and Jhajharia trained smart, racked their brains for the best way forward and remained undeterred by what might have sounded like radio silence from their countrymen in response to their exhilarating efforts in their early days. The two would leverage as much science as they could access. Mariyappan's, on the other hand, was the ultimate inspirational story of wanting to shake off a humble financial situation and pull his mother, a vegetable vendor, out of the clutches of grim poverty.

A confidence crisis was never too far off for each of them, but they would talk their bodies and minds out of the thought of giving up, and keep chipping away at the enormity of the challenge. No severed limb or weakened torso could pull them back from the self-belief they etched into the wall of granite-carved grit. Every small movement, every inch of progress added to their resolve as hurling a javelin to make it fly assumed the wonder of magic, their wands guided by a mind that never entertained a *No*.

~

It's the mammoth might of the country now, in fact, that refuses to accept listless results in sport. 2016 saw the twin successes of Sindhu and Sakshi, but Rio also brought to the surface the restlessness that gnaws at the country when medals dry up. India doesn't take No's any more.

Nor is India any more a country that watches one brief spot of a dazzle, resigned to watching the sport fading away. Gone are the days when P.T. Usha and Malleswari and Leander Paes and Gopichand and Sania Mirza and Dingko Singh were one-offs. Every sport is now looking for a pack of contenders, a system that will deliver a multipronged charge at medals rather than heaping all hopes on to one pair of shoulders.

With improved scientific expertise, a stream of funders, such as corporates, stepping in with a tad more enthusiasm and endless individual drive, Indian athletes are taking incremental steps and pushing boundaries further. A smattering of tennis singles players, a brand-new bunch of track and field athletes, the ultra-competitive shuttlers racing each other and a clutch of talented teen shooters mean the country has now awakened from its slumber. When the chrysalis gets shrugged off, India's athletes will show they can fly without wings. Or at least soar while trying.

Abhijeet Kulkarni is a sports journalist who has been covering badminton for almost two decades now. Apart from his writing on sports and other sociopolitical issues, he has also been involved in the identification and nurturing of sports talent at the grass-roots level, earlier with an NGO and now in an individual capacity.

6

Indian Badminton: From Also-Rans to Champions

Abhijeet Kulkarni

The indoor hall at the Gachibowli Stadium, Hyderabad, was all decked up for the biggest badminton tournament it had ever hosted, with the who's who of world badminton scheduled to showcase their skills over the next one week.

On one of the side courts, three women in black-and-red kits were busy mopping the playing surface before their team was scheduled to start its practice session; almost every eye in the stadium was glued to the trio answering to the names of 2008 Olympic champion Zhang Ning, two-time world champion Xie Xingfang and the pre-tournament favourite Lu Lan.

In the other corner, the Indian team minus Saina Nehwal was beginning its warm-up and the obvious question in the mind of every Indian present in the stands was whether the country's top stars would ever command that kind of attention.

Saina, a year earlier, had made the world stand up and take notice when she reached the women's singles quarterfinals in the 2008 Beijing Olympics and then went on to become the first Indian shuttler to be crowned Junior World Champion. And even though the Indian media was billing the 2009 World Championship on her home turf as the Saina versus China battle, everyone knew that India's shuttle queen was still a rank outsider, with the recent bout of chicken pox only hurting her prospects.

Exactly nine years later, with China hosting the 2018 World Championship, the tide seemed to have turned. Indian women have won at least one medal in the sport's biggest events—World Championship or the Olympics—since 2011, while the Chinese women have failed to win a single major title for over eighteen months.

But the heartiest thing about the decade gone by is that the India story has gone much beyond a Saina or a Sindhu, with the country's badminton stars achieving many historic firsts and taking firm steps towards making the nation a true world badminton powerhouse.

Saina and Kidambi Srikanth became the first Indian men and women badminton players, respectively, to climb the summit of the official BWF world ranking ladder in 2015 and 2018, with the latter becoming, in 2017, only the fourth men's singles player to win four Superseries titles in a calendar year.

In the team events, India's mixed team won its first gold in the 2018 Commonwealth Games, apart from winning a medal in four of the five individual events, the women's team bagged an Uber Cup and an Asian Games bronze in 2014, Jwala Gutta and Ashwini Ponnappa bagged a women's doubles bronze in the 2011 World Championship, and in 2017, Saina and Sindhu finished on the women's singles podium together as India won two medals in a single edition of the championship for the first time.

That is not to say that Indian badminton stars before this current lot did not achieve any success on the international scene. The legendary Prakash Padukone was one of the dominant figures on the international circuit in the early 1980s, India won multiple medals in the 1982 Asian Games, Aparna Popat became the first Indian finalist in the World Juniors in 1996, and a certain Dinesh Khanna still holds the record for being the only senior Indian Asian Champion, a title he won back in 1965.

But there is no denying the fact that the past decade has finally seen the profile of Indian badminton rise from a nation with skilful players but little success to a breeding ground of potential champions whom the world has come to fear.

Seeds sown in 2001

What marked that shift in momentum could be Saina's unexpected run to the 2008 Beijing Olympics quarterfinals, where she came within ten points of reaching a medal round against Indonesia's Maria Kristin Yulianti but could not hold her nerves in the decider.

But the seeds of that shift were probably sown seven years before that, when the current chief national coach and the man who is credited with the rise of Indian badminton ended the country's twenty-one-year wait for the coveted All England title.

In 1994, Pullela Gopichand had suffered a horrendous knee injury that required multiple surgeries only to ensure that he played again. But instead of taking it as a signal to look beyond badminton and make a career somewhere else, the five-time national champion decided to take the more challenging route of marrying the Indian skill sets with the power and fitness approach of the East Asians and stood atop the podium in the most prestigious badminton tournament in the world.

Gopi, as he is popularly known in badminton circles, has time and again spoken about the body aches and ice baths required to merely recover for the next match during the tournament. The narrative of how things happened through that week in Birmingham still gives goosebumps even to repeat listeners.The year 2001 was the last time the All England was played on a cement court. The hard surface was an additional challenge for Gopichand, given the career-threatening knee injury he had suffered a few years ago. With no physiotherapist or masseur to help him with his recovery, Gopi would rely on ice baths and stretching to prepare for the next match.

But more than the hardships that he went through, the real takeaway from that triumph for Gopi was probably the understanding that Indians could challenge the world's best if they worked on their strength and fitness. It was that understanding that sowed the seeds of success that Indian badminton is currently witnessing.

Never shy of speaking his mind, albeit in the softest of voices possible, Gopi even ripped into his compatriots after winning the Syed Modi All India Ranking tournament a few years later, stating that if they could not beat a man like him who was struggling with injuries, then they had no chance of making it big on the international stage.

It wasn't a case of dearth of talent on the Indian domestic circuit. The likes of Chetan Anand, Anup Sridhar and Abhinn Shyam Gupta were perfectly capable of beating anyone in their day, but they would run out of steam going into the business end of even mid-level tournaments. Even nine-time national champion Aparna Popat has admitted a few times that it was the lack of strength that hurt her on the international circuit and she felt that had anyone taken care of that aspect of her training at an early age, she could have achieved a lot more.

For Gopi, the missing link between Indian players carrying the also-ran tag and actually winning the major titles was the lack of fitness and hunger to do everything needed to win those big medals. And, as a coach, he wanted to create a system that would eventually bridge that gap.

This writer has been privy to many conversations between the former All England Champion and senior players soon after he took over as the Chief National Coach in 2006 about the need to win that one big title for which they would be remembered, instead of just focusing on safeguarding their rankings and qualifying for the big events.

It was a period of acrimony in Indian badminton. Gopi wanted to stop the players from entering tournaments till they were fit enough to make a mark in those events, while the top stars were worried that such a strategy would hurt their chances of qualifying for the 2008 Beijing Olympics.

There were differences between the coach and a group of senior players, including, among others, Chetan Anand, Jwala Gutta and Shruti Kurien, over restrictions on participating in international tournaments and Gopi's insistence on them spending more time in the national camp to improve strength and fitness. This ultimately led to a media circus, and while Gopi did try to explain his viewpoint for a while, he decided to shut out all distractions and start working on the junior bunch, which had started making some waves in the domestic circuit. It definitely helped that most of them were part of his academy, which had started with a summer camp at the Jubilee Hills Club in Hyderabad in 2003.

The Journey of Gopichand Badminton Academy

With injuries affecting his playing career, Gopi had already started helping youngsters training with him, and the first batch of his summer camp was a mix of upcoming talent, including Saina, P. Kashyap and Guru Sai Dutt, and beginners, including Sindhu, among others. Buoyed by the response to the camp, he decided to start a regular batch a few months later.

While starting an academy wasn't the difficult part, the real challenge was creating the infrastructure that has come to provide India so many champions.

Having seen the facilities abroad during his playing days, and the challenges he faced back home due to the lack of proper infrastructure and support systems, Gopi had already made up his mind to create a world-class academy after retirement and had used his 2001 title triumph to procure a piece of land from the Andhra Pradesh government.

But that was just the start of a long challenge. It took Gopi almost a year and a half to locate a piece of land and complete the necessary documentation for his future project, despite the support of Chief Minister Chandrababu Naidu and some well-meaning officials in various ministries.

And even though he was seeking about 5 acres of space for the academy, he finally had to settle for two plots close to each other. Something that worked for him in the future. But more on that later.

Getting the project up and running was the next big challenge, as Gopi's attempt to raise funds through sponsorship mostly fired blanks. A high-ranking official in a public sector unit even made him wait for hours for a meeting before telling him that badminton wasn't a sport with much of a future in India and that there was no point investing in it.

These rejections, according to Gopi, have been his biggest driving force, as he was determined to prove the doubters wrong. It was Andhra businessman Nimmagadda Prasad who initially gave Rs 2 crore for the academy. Many more sponsors joined in as the actual construction started in 2005. But as costs escalated, Gopi had to mortgage his house and put most of his life savings in building the academy, with Prasad bailing him out on a couple of more occasions.

The academy was finally inaugurated in June 2008, only to face its biggest hurdle till date when the Y.S.R. Reddy government issued a notice to reclaim 2.5 acres of land to build a sports school three months later. The logic was—a badminton academy doesn't need a swimming pool or an athletics track and hence the land could be put to better use ahead of the 2012 London Olympics.

The government never explained the rationale behind the order or what their actual plans were, but Gopi took them to court and instead of waiting for the verdict, went for broke by completing the work for the swimming pool and other facilities at the earliest.

While these teething troubles would have bogged down any other individual or organization and affected their efficiency, Gopi, along with his mother, Subbaravamma, ensured that the academy became a supply line for world-class talent.

With Gopi's wife, P.V.V. Lakshmi, herself an Olympian, busy with her job and household responsibilities, Subbaravamma took upon herself the administrative responsibilities of the academy, keeping an eye on the minute details required to provide the best of facilities to the players and also becoming a sort of mentor to the girls and boys who were staying away from their family. This allowed Gopi to concentrate on coaching and other important issues, ensuring that the seeds that were sown back in April 2004, with a coaching staff of four, including Mohammad Siddiqui (Siadutt), J. Rajendra Kumar and

Govardhan Reddy apart from himself, grew into a successful enterprise that produced champions.

Gopi and his team of coaches brought in a refreshing change to the system as they began involving themselves in the players' training, overall development and even personal issues to ensure that nothing affected their focus and training.

The kind of control Gopi exerted on his trainees wasn't easy for all to handle. As Saina began to make a mark on the international stage, stories of how the coach banned her from eating her favourite aloo paratha and ice cream and introduced her to non-vegetarian food started doing the rounds.

So, one day during the 2008 Junior World Championship campaign in Pune, I happened to speak to the man himself about it.

'How much do you control Saina?'

And the reply was, 'I need to even know the number of times she goes to the loo.'[1]

His hands-on approach to coaching, planning sessions and even rests, down to the minutest detail, and a strict vigil on every player's on- and off-court activities soon began to bear fruit, with Saina and P. Kashyap starting to challenge the seniors in the domestic circuit within a year.

The academy also roped in the services of Tom John, a London-based coach of Indian origin, who would travel with the two to domestic tournaments while the other coaching staff looked after the youngsters back in Hyderabad.

The Badminton Association of India's (BAI) decision to make him the chief national coach in 2006, after U. Vimal Kumar decided to step down after a successful stint, meant that Gopi now had more power and opportunity to plan the future of the country's upcoming stars, as the national camps were also shifted to Hyderabad.

Yes, there were teething troubles in trying to implement his ideology, with the senior shuttlers unwilling to adjust to the national coach's methods, but slowly and surely, the results of his trainees and the younger crop of players began to shut out the dissenting voices.

Saina was the flag-bearer of the new generation, winning two national titles and the Level 4 Philippines Open even before turning sixteen, and had clearly started becoming the darling of sports fans across the country before she qualified for the 2008 Beijing Olympics.

But that hardly merited any preferential treatment for the star shuttler back at the academy, the operations of which had by then shifted to its first state-of-the-art facility a few kilometres away from the Gachibowli stadium.

Gopi, who insists that there is no place for democracy if one has to produce champions, imposed a curfew after 7 p.m. for anyone staying in the academy. The lights had to be out by 10 p.m., and anyone wanting to leave the premises any time during the day needed written permission from the boss himself, or else the security would not let them go out. To add to this, there was a limit on the time any player could use her/his phone, and the forty-four-year-old would, many a time, make surprise visits to the rooms or the eating area to ensure that every instruction was being followed to the T.

While not everyone was amused by the strict rules and clamping down on the players' freedom of movement, many admit that the drive of their coach rubbed off on everyone. For Gopi, the day would start around 4 a.m., as he would meditate and spend a bit of 'me time' before heading to the academy for a session at 5.30 a.m. Even that early-morning personal time was cut short once Sindhu began to make a mark and needed more personalized attention from the coach.

The demands of coaching a bunch of players who were already beginning to make a mark on the national and international circuits ultimately resulted in Gopi shifting out of his house in Jubilee Hills to a rented place near the academy to reduce the time spent on travelling.

He also understood the importance of holding more international tournaments in India to provide exposure to the youngsters. He took on the additional responsibility of organizing a Grand Prix Gold–level event in Hyderabad and the 2009 World Championship, before the Union government decided to pump in a lot of money for preparations ahead of the 2010 Commonwealth Games in New Delhi, and that simply fast-tracked the progress of Indian badminton.

As things stand now, the academy has become a centre of excellence, with national camps being held around the year and over 600 kids training across two centres in Hyderabad, one in Noida and one in Vadodara.

The Sports Authority of India, in collaboration with the Gopichand Academy, has created a permanent centre in the second structure, built about a kilometre away from the first, with the financial help of the sports ministry on the 1-acre land that was separately allotted to Gopi back in 2001.

The two centres, equipped with seventeen courts, accommodate around 100 players, with over fifteen coaches and a dozen physiotherapists and trainers working with them through the day, while the office staff is busy fending off almost 500 calls a month, telling parents that admissions for even the beginners' batch are overflowing and they would have to wait for at least six months before calling back again.

The Decade of Saina Nehwal

The face of this transformation has undoubtedly been Saina Nehwal. The teenager with a boy cut, slightly oversized shorts and complete disdain for the reputation of her opponents had started making her mark on the national and international scene by 2005, but it was three years later that she made the world of badminton take notice of India's potential on the biggest stage possible.

Saina had already created history for Indian badminton, having won the four-star Philippines Open and emulating Popat by reaching the Junior World Championship finals in 2006. And though she had been making steady progress thereafter, it was in the heart of the Chinese capital that the then eighteen-year-old showed what she was capable of, by almost reaching the semi-finals of the 2008 Olympics.

The unseeded Indian upset fourth seed and 2007 World Championship silver medallist Chen Wang of Hong Kong in the third round and was leading 11-3 in the decider in the quarterfinals against eventual bronze medallist Maria Kristin Yulianti of Indonesia, when nerves got the better of her and she could win only three of the next twenty-one points before she lost the match.

Gopi loves to tell the story of how he tried to cheer up a distraught Saina on the way back by telling her that the next day's training session would begin at 6 a.m., and while he was expecting her to ask for a break, all she asked was for the session to start at 6.30 a.m.

The often-repeated story probably epitomizes the single-mindedness Saina possessed towards the game. The eighteen-year-old created history a few months later when she went on to become the first Indian World Junior champion in Pune, and in December, broke into the World Top 10 where she stayed for almost a decade.

Saina's list of firsts will be a lesson in the history of Indian badminton. The girl from Hyderabad was the first Indian woman to win any title above the satellite category, the first Superseries champion, the first Olympic medallist and the first to reach World No. 1, which she did in 2015.

But more than these firsts, the two-time World Championship medallist was the catalyst for change that Indian badminton had never seen before.

Before the emergence of Saina, Indian badminton players, with probably the respectable exceptions of Prakash Padukone, Aparna Popat and Gopi himself, rarely believed that they had the quality to go out and win tournaments.

Most of them were happy making the grade of representing the country in major events and were more obsessed with maintaining their rankings to qualify for these events rather than aiming for anything bigger.

Any chat about the draw or their chances in major tournaments would start and end with talk of what stage of the tournament they were likely to face a Chinese or an opponent from any major badminton nation.

Saina was a contrast to that approach. Even as a fourteen-year-old, when she began playing in the senior domestic circuit, the stocky youngster with a boyish haircut would hardly mince words and proclaim that she would beat the seniors rather easily, because 'I train a lot harder than them.'

Her statements then would attract the charge of arrogance. However, in a year or two, she showed that she could not just overpower these seniors but also create a career path that none of them had even envisaged.

She won back-to-back Nationals in 2006–07 and then, instead of targeting Popat's record of nine titles, she decided to look beyond—at international glory.

Within the next four years, she had surpassed the nine-time national champion and first Indian to reach the World Junior Championship finals, by winning the crown on her second attempt. Not only that, she also went on to become the only challenger to Chinese hegemony by the time the 2012 London Olympics arrived.

As things stand, the twenty-eight-year-old who returned to the Nationals in 2017 and won the title for the third time has an Olympic bronze, a World Championship silver and a bronze, ten Superseries titles, and two Commonwealth Games individual gold medals.

And despite suffering a career-threatening knee injury, and the emergence of many talented youngsters on the world scene, she is still considered one of India's best bets for a medal at the Tokyo 2020 Olympic Games.

For a considerable period of this decade, Saina was the lone warrior for India on the international circuit, with the mixed doubles combination of Jwala Gutta and V. Diju, and later, the women's doubles pairing of Jwala and Ashwini Ponnappa, achieving some noteworthy results.

Though Jwala and Diju ended up breaking into the World Top 10 and even played the summit clash of the year-ending BWF Finals, they never really challenged for titles in major international events.

Aditi Mutatkar, who was Saina's contemporary and India No. 2 behind the star shuttler for a considerable amount of time, had once told this writer about how it was because of Saina's exploits that they started believing that even they could achieve something big in life.

Aditi had, by then, undergone two knee surgeries, and not many gave her a chance to sustain for long on the gruelling international circuit. But she managed to reach a career-high ranking of 27 and could have become the second Indian woman after Saina to win a Grand Prix-level title in 2008, had she converted any of the 10 match points she had in the Bitburger Open final against Maria Febe Kusumastuti.

Just like she was for Aditi, Saina became an inspiration for not just the next generation but also for those who had grown up with her or were even a bit senior to her.

More importantly, she has inspired thousands of young kids to take up the sport and look at it as a career option. The national and state ranking age-group tournaments today boast entries regularly touching the 1000 mark, and much credit for this change definitely goes to the success of Saina and the others who have followed in her footsteps in the last decade.

There is one name that definitely deserves prominent mention—Jwala Gutta. The outspoken left-hander from Hyderabad was the sole reason Indian doubles got any attention from fans and authorities.

There are many who like to question her ranting against the system and compare her achievements to Saina's. But one cannot deny that despite all limitations, she forged a path of her own with Diju in mixed doubles and Ashwini in women's doubles.

While Jwala and Diju blazed a trail for Indians in mixed doubles, Jwala and Ashwini went a few steps further when they clinched the 2010 Commonwealth Games women's doubles gold medal, and then ended India's twenty-eight-year wait for a World Championship medal a year later, in London, with a bronze-winning performance.

It was a period when Indian badminton turned over a new leaf, with Saina completing a hat-trick of titles in BWF tournaments, India winning two golds, a team silver, the men's singles bronze in the 2010 Commonwealth Games in New Delhi, H.S. Prannoy winning a silver in the inaugural Youth Olympics, and then Jwala and Ashwini topping it off with a World Championship medal at the Wembley Arena.

Indian badminton hasn't looked back since then, with a new crop of badminton stars, including the likes of Prannoy, Kidambi Srikanth, Ajay Jayaram and B. Sai Praneeth taking over the mantle from Chetan Anand and company in the men's singles department, while Saina and Sindhu have been challenging and pushing each other to achieve bigger successes.

The emergence of Sindhu did create a few problems at the Gopichand Badminton Academy, with its most prominent pupil deciding to move out in 2014 for more personalized attention.

While many questioned Saina's wisdom in moving to Bengaluru to train under Vimal Kumar, the decision did pay dividends for the twenty-eight-year-old, who found a new spring in her stride as she became the first Indian ever to climb the World Ranking summit in 2015. She was looking good for another Olympic medal in 2016, but a knee injury put paid to her hopes.

To the delight of Indian fans, though, Sindhu stepped up to the challenge, bagging a silver medal in Rio.

While the two Indian shuttle queens—who are also being supported by the Olympic Gold Quest—were taking flight, a new crop of men's singles players was also looking to make a move. It definitely helped that the likes of GoSports Foundation came forward to support these up-and-coming stars and provide the much-needed backup to the efforts of the sports ministry and the BAI.

It was a small initiative that started back in 2008, but the financial and technical support that the likes of Srikanth, Prannoy, Sameer and Sourabh Verma and

G. Ruthvika Shivani got in their formative days ensured that they got enough international exposure early in their career and have now started achieving the kind of success that was envisaged by the founding members of the foundation.

Srikanth, the twenty-five-year-old from Guntur, is undoubtedly the biggest success story of that initiative. Known as a doubles specialist during his junior days, the Gopichand Academy trainee surprised everyone in 2014 by beating the legendary Lin Dan on his home turf to clinch the China Open title and become the first Indian men's singles player to clinch a Superseries title.

Despite a few ups and downs in his career, which also saw injuries and meningitis slow his progress, Srikanth has gone from strength to strength and become only the third men's singles player to win four Superseries titles in a calendar year in 2017 and reach the World No. 1 spot in 2018.

Prannoy has also broken into the World Top 10 and has the Asian Championship bronze medal to show for his effort, apart from a couple of Grand Prix Gold titles. The sports science interventions from the experts working with them have played a major part in their development and injury management, given the added stress on their bodies brought about by the way the sport is played now.

While the journey of the last ten years has been extremely satisfying, the real challenge will be to not just sustain the development but also build on the foundation to produce more champions.

The one area where there is huge scope for development is in the doubles categories. Since Jwala's retirement, the women's doubles pairs have struggled to make a mark on the circuit. However, the men's doubles category has started to look up, thanks to the exploits of Satwiksairaj Rankireddy and Chirag Shetty on the Superseries circuit.

But these are merely baby steps compared to the revolution in singles, and it is important that the BAI and the likes of GoSports Foundation, Olympic Gold Quest, and other, similar organizations spend more money and energy in identifying and nurturing doubles talent from an early age.

However, the bigger challenge for everyone involved in the sport is to spread the net wide and create uniform systems across the country to produce more champions.

In the last few years, many former players like Aravind Bhat, Chetan Anand and Nikhil Kanetkar, and the state associations of Assam and Uttar Pradesh have started their own academies. Even the Prakash Padukone Badminton Academy, the first real finishing school in the country, has started concentrating on the juniors, and many, including Lakshya Sen and Aakarshi Kashyap, have started finding their feet in the senior circuit.

Over the last decade, the number of players in competitive badminton has suddenly exploded, with the BAI forced to change its tournament structure in 2018—holding U-19 and U-13 All India Ranking tournaments as independent events—to ensure that the tournaments get over within a week.

Despite that, organizers have been complaining about the challenges of managing the events, which are attracting more than 1000 entries in each age category.

The BAI's initiative of creating a professional league—Premier Badminton League—on the lines of the Indian Premier League to try and attract more corporate support has managed to make the sport more popular. The apex body also has plans to launch a junior league on the same lines with an aim to provide more exposure to junior players.

But as Gopichand says, what India has done so far isn't sustainable unless we manage to institutionalize the systems that created champions over the past ten years, and the focus going forward should be on creating quality coaches and support systems.

There is, after all, no dearth of talent in India. Gopi has shown that proper planning and mentoring can convert that talent into champions. Now the next step would be to turn India into a badminton powerhouse, and every stakeholder will have to pull up their socks to achieve that goal in the coming decade.

go!

Roopa Pai is the author of several books for children, including the much-acclaimed, award-winning bestseller *The Gita For Children*. Her books, on themes as varied as sci-fi fantasy, history, popular science, mathematics, economics, life skills and philosophy, are enjoyed by adults just as much as they are by children. This computer engineer is also a TEDx speaker and co-founder of the heritage walks and tours company Bangalore Walks. She plays no sport at all but is a dedicated follower of several, especially those that involve Indian sportswomen and/or Rafa Nadal.

7

Baadal Pe Paaon Hai: A Fan's Journey through the Rise and Rise of the Indian Sportswoman

Roopa Pai

8 August 1984, four days before the closing ceremony of the glittering 23rd Summer Olympics at Los Angeles. The finals of the women's 400-metre hurdles—, featuring, in Lane 5, the very first Indian woman in the finals of any Olympic event, ever—are about to be flagged off. The starting pistol goes, and the twenty-year-old in Lane 5, conscious that she is carrying the hopes of an entire sports-mad, non-sporting nation on her tall, angular frame, begins strongly, but pulls up two seconds in. Someone has made a false start, and the race must be restarted.

Her focus a little shaken, the girl returns to the starting blocks and forces herself to concentrate. The previous day, she had run the semi-final heats at 55.54, and won the heats (a feat that no other Indian woman Olympic athlete has been able to repeat in the almost thirty-five years since), forcing the American television commentator to sit up and take notice, to acknowledge that 'Yoosha' was one of the favourites, not just for a podium finish, but—hold your breath—a gold medal.

The pistol goes off again, and this time there's no looking back. The girl runs the race of her life, stopping the clock at 55.42, and setting, in the process, a national record that stands to this day, but it proves to be a hundredth of a second too late to make the kind of history she had hoped to. It is a heartbreaking repeat of another fourth-place finish, that one a quarter of a century earlier, at the 1960 Rome Olympics, where the Indian contender, Milkha Singh, had finished a tenth of a second behind that bronze medal winner.

'I cried and cried, for days,' chuckles the fifty-four-year-old, at the memory of her distraught younger self, in a recent interview.[1] You cannot help but marvel at that chuckle—so light, so free of bitterness and rancour, so lacking the shadow of regret one would expect from an athlete who scaled every peak that she essayed in her personal quest for sporting excellence. Every peak, that is to say, bar one.

The lightness of Usha's chuckle—for, of course, we have been talking of none other than the Payyoli Express, our Golden Girl, the great P.T. Usha—stands out particularly sharply when seen against the background of the collective hand-wringing and breast-beating the country put itself through after the 1984 Olympics, when the Indian squad—a lean, mean contingent of only forty-eight of our best, pruned down from the seventy-six that had been sent to the much-boycotted Moscow Games four years earlier—returned with no medals at all. The unkindest cut was that the much-touted men's hockey team, which had won gold at eight Olympics, including Moscow, had placed a humiliating fifth. (To rub salt into the LA wound, Pakistan won the gold.)

The self-loathing was particularly acute because of what had gone before. Just two years earlier, national pride had touched an all-time high after the success of the 1982 Delhi Asian Games, which had seen the capital transformed and brought in world-class sporting infrastructure and international coaches in droves for the benefit of Indian sportspeople. That pride, further bolstered by India's fifty-seven-medal haul, had ensured that expectations from the contingent that went to the 1984 Games had reached stratospheric—and quite unreasonable—heights. Plus, in 1983, Kapil Dev's men had won the cricket World Cup, sending hopes soaring even further. After all, if we could be world-beaters in cricket, it was only a matter of time—like, say, a year—before we turned world-beaters in every other sport!

The let-down, when it came, therefore, was eviscerating. The fact that the country had, at the exact same time, also entered the brave new era of television-watching, with events being beamed directly into Indian living rooms, did not help. For the first time, Indians saw, with their own eyes, how far behind the rest of the world our athletes stood, what a long, long way we had still to go to create the

kind of infrastructure that would help raise a generation
of world-beating sportspeople, and, in the absence of any
effective formal system by which to 'catch 'em young', by
what a rum chance an athlete of Usha's natural genius had
been found at all.

~

I was thirteen when the LA Games—and Usha's Olympic
dream—went down. All around me, post an all-too-brief
dalliance with optimism, adults were falling back, almost
with a sense of relief, into the comfort zone of their
favourite pastime—dissing the country, despairing about
Usha ever being able to make anything of herself. Luckily,
our sporting merits as a nation (or the lack of them, as had
been amply displayed) did not affect me, a nerdy teenager
who had no sporting talent and who routinely skived off PE
(physical education) class begging a stomach ache, in quite
the same way. Seeing how close an Indian woman—who
had done nothing more than follow her coach's injunctions
to the letter, work very, very hard, and believe in herself—
had gotten to an Olympic medal impacted me in a different
way. It turned me into a lifelong fan.

I noticed, therefore, other stories, about Indian female
athletes, that got buried in the depressing post-Olympics
analysis, and in the other awful events of a particularly
Orwellian 1984.

Did you know, for instance, that eighteen-year-old
Shiny Abraham (now Wilson) became the first Indian
woman to qualify for an Olympic track and field semi-final

when she made the cut in the 800 metres at LA, the day before Usha did the same in her event? I did, and tom-tommed it to whoever would listen. Shiny would not make the final, but she would go on to achieve other unique distinctions in the future, including becoming the only female Indian athlete to participate in four—that's right, four—Olympics. At the opening ceremony of her penultimate Olympics—Barcelona, 1992—she became the first woman to win the honour of marching at the head of the Indian contingent.

(Let's press the pause button for a moment here. Let's reflect on the fact that the Olympics is a circus of extraordinary 'freaks', and that just qualifying for it catapults an athlete into the 'superhuman' category. It might help put the enormity of Shiny's achievement—qualifying for four successive Olympics—into perspective.)

Here's another story from LA. Did you know that the first Indian relay team to ever make an Olympic final did so in the 4x400-metre relay at the 1984 Games, and comprised the crack team of Kerala girls—Usha, Shiny and M.D. Valsamma—along with (and my jingoistic heart always swells a little at this point) Karnataka's own Vandana Rao? Well, I knew that story too.

Shiny remembers the high of that fortnight very well.

'I was not sad at all to lose the 800-metre semi-final— qualifying itself was good enough for me,' she said in an interview some years ago. '[As for the relay] . . . it was such a shock for everyone there in the US to see Indian girls in an athletics final! It was a great Olympics for all of us girls.'[2]

The rest of the eighties, and part of the nineties, were all about Indian women in track and field athletics; in this department of sport at least, the men did not figure at all in public consciousness. With local icons and a culture of 'women who run and jump' taking root, the south continued to be the fertile ground that birthed the country's champion female athletes, year after year, ATF meet after ATF meet, Asian Games after Asian Games. I followed their fortunes as they did their country proud on the international stage—not just the four women mentioned earlier, but also sprinters Vandana Shanbhag, Kutty Saramma and Ashwini Nachappa (in 1990, Ashwini beat Usha in the 200 metres, not once but twice, becoming more famous for that than for her other, considerable achievements, including three golds in the SAF Games in Pakistan in 1988, for instance), heptathlete Reeth Abraham, long jumpers Mercy Kuttan and Anju Bobby George, and long-distance runners Geeta Zutshi and Suman Rawat.

But while the 1986 Asian Games in Seoul returned a rich haul of wins, helping India retain the fifth place in the overall tally of medals it had first gained for itself in 1982 (four of the five gold medals we won in Seoul had our brave girls' names on them, including three individual ones for Usha and a fourth for the members of the same relay team that had made the final in LA), and while the Asian Track & Field Meets provided our athletes some good pickings, success at the Olympics, and even the other Asian Games, continued to elude them. In fact, Olympic success eluded the men too. The medal drought that began in LA would continue for a dozen years, all the way until

1996, in Atlanta, when Leander Paes would become only the second Indian man in a hundred years to bring home a medal, a bronze, in an individual event. (The other was K.D. Jadhav, who won the bronze medal in freestyle wrestling in Helsinki in 1952.)

What was perhaps more worrying was the fact that the supply of international-level track and field athletes seemed to be drying up, belying the promise that had been held out so tantalizingly in the eighties. More importantly, despite all the schemes to identify talent at the grass-roots levels that the government had set up, other sporting disciplines hadn't yet thrown up any female rock stars.

~

Meanwhile, at a different level, in a different arena, all was changing, changing utterly. In 1990, India finally shook off the shackles of its protectionist economy and opened its doors to the world. To the generation of urban Indians that turned twenty in the nineties—read: me and everyone a few years younger—the metamorphosis of everything that was familiar and predictable, and the pace at which the change was happening, was nothing short of mind-blowing. All around us, sprouting like a rash, was the terrible beauty of glass-and-chrome malls, featuring international brands that we had only encountered—and not-so-secretly coveted—inside the seductive suitcases of NRI relatives. Suddenly, we had at our fingertips, via something called the World Wide Web, free, full and instant access to the collective knowledge of humankind, never mind that we had to use a slow and unreliable dial-up modem to get to it. We had adulted into a glittering world of undreamt-of salaries, foreign travel for leisure, and conspicuous, continuous McConsumption.

We learnt gleefully the revolutionary concept of something called disposable income, and understood that it was okay not to salt away every last penny for a rainy day, as our parents had done. Encouraged by the relaxing of the government's stranglehold on industry and enterprise, we began to cautiously entertain the idea of being entrepreneurs—people who did things purely for profit—without feeling vaguely dirty about it. With access to international television programming, we had white people every day in our own living rooms; we knew now how they talked and dressed, what they loved to eat, what music they listened to, what they cared about, how they won (or did not win) at things, what they did right (and what we could, therefore, get right too).

That knowledge demolished many of our unarticulated fears and feelings of inferiority when it came to the 'developed world', bestowing upon us the first definite spark of a world-beating confidence our parents had never had, alongside the goosebump-inducing realization that the world had suddenly become far more of a level playing field than ever before. That devil-may-care chutzpah was what impelled my contemporary, twenty-one-year-old former athlete and Miss India Madhu Sapre, to declare, in response to a judge's question in the finals of the Miss Universe 1992 pageant, about what she would do if she became prime minister of India for a year: 'I will build a world-class sports stadium.'[3] That straight-from-the-heart 'sportswoman's answer' would cause her to get endlessly trolled back home and cost her the crown—she would have stood a better chance if she had expressed a resolve to build hospitals or orphanages or put poverty-eradication programmes in place—but the fact that she said what she did, and stood by her answer after the event, only served to underscore the change that was sweeping across the land.

It was a heady, heady time. We were 100 per cent certain that our lives, and more so, our children's, were going to be far shinier, far happier and certainly far, far more exciting than our parents'.

If this was the experience of their parents, imagine the suitably amplified impact this confident, optimistic, hungry new India would have had on the children, especially the girls, who were born in the nineties, or a little earlier!

Let's just talk about some of those girls, shall we, girls born in the ten-year window between 1985 and 1995? Let's talk about Kavita Raut (b.1985), Sania Mirza (b.1986), Joshna Chinappa (b.1986), Sudha Singh (b.1986), Tania Sachdev (b.1986), Koneru Humpy (b.1987), Ashwini Akkunji (b.1987), Geeta Phogat (b.1988), Babita Kumari Phogat (b.1989), Heena Sidhu (b.1989), Ashwini Ponnappa (b.1989), Tintu Luka (b.1989), Lalita Babar (b.1989), Rahi Sarnobat (b.1990), Pinki Rani Jangra (b.1990) and Saina Nehwal (b.1990). Let's talk about Dipika Pallikal (b.1991), Ritu Rani (b.1991), Sakshi Malik (b.1992), Dipa Karmakar (b.1993), Deepika Kumari (b.1994), Rani Rampal (b.1994), Vinesh Phogat (b.1994),

Mirabai Chanu (b.1994), P.V. Sindhu (b.1995) and Manika Batra (b.1995). Let's talk about the range of different sports—tennis, squash, wrestling, weightlifting, boxing, shooting, steeplechase, chess, badminton, gymnastics, archery, hockey, table tennis—that these girls are representing their country in, and winning, at all kinds of international forums. Let's talk about how fantastical, how far-fetched, this story would have seemed back in 1990, to the twenty-year-old me.

~

But not just yet. Let's leave these girls to their childhoods for now, and talk instead of the ones who led the charge into the brave new millennium of Indian sport. Because, really, the big change began in the year 2000, at the Sydney Olympics. Indians remember Sydney as the Games when a twenty-five-year-old from a small weightlifters' village in the Andhra backwaters hefted a nation's hopes skywards, and became the first Indian woman to snatch an Olympic medal, a bronze. Her name was Karnam Malleswari. What many do not remember was that this braveheart was expecting to win gold.

It wasn't too far-fetched an expectation, either—by the time Sydney rolled around, Malleswari had made world-beating a habit. In 1993, when she was only eighteen, she had won her first international medal, a bronze, at the World Championships. She followed it up with a gold and a world record in '94, another gold in '95, and India's first silver in the sport at the Asian Games in 1994.

In case you're wondering, no, Malleswari was not part of the Indian squad at Atlanta 1996. How come? Well, simply because women's weightlifting wasn't yet an Olympic sport—it debuted only in Sydney. If this hadn't been the case, there may well have been other women in the Atlanta contingent, including almost certainly the diminutive Kunjarani Devi, who had been runner-up in her category at no less than seven World Championships since 1989, well before Malleswari entered the arena!

But back to the Sydney Games. Apart from our medal winner, two other women had quietly stamped their presence there. Sixteen years after Usha and Shiny had entered the semi-finals of an Olympic sprint event, K.M. Beenamol became the third to do so, in the 400 metres. The other, Anjali Bhagwat, who had made a huge splash at the Commonwealth Championships the previous year, winning three golds and one silver, became the first to enter the Olympic last eight in a sport that no Indian woman had ever participated in at the international level—the 10-metre air pistol. She would go on to win on the international stage again and again, even becoming World No. 1 in 2002.

~

The trouble, then as now, is that no sporting achievement, save in a few sports, such as tennis or chess, captures public imagination as instantly or as dazzlingly as an Olympic medal. Perhaps it was that realization that prompted two world-beating non-Olympians to come together in the year of the Sydney Games to conceive of a non-profit with an audacious single-point vision—to help a country that had won no more than three individual medals in half a century of the Olympics to go for nothing less than gold. Six-time winner of the billiards Pro World Championships Geet Sethi, who had seen first-hand the problems that plagued Indian sport when he was part of the Asian Games contingent in 1998 (he had won a gold and a silver there), joined hands with legendary former badminton World No. 1 Prakash Padukone to launch, in 2002, what they called simply, Olympic Gold Quest. The plan was to raise money from private sources and provide every kind of support that Indian athletes needed to pursue their Olympic dreams.

But Olympic dreams need time, patience and an enormous amount of collective national effort and will before they begin to bear fruit. By the turn of the millennium, however, there was no doubt in anyone's mind that the biggest barrier to Indian sporting success— not infrastructure, not international coaches, not world-class equipment, not talent, but the lack of self-belief that we could be world-beaters—was slowly beginning to be breached. The low rumble of confidence that had made itself heard at Sydney turned into a roar at the 2002 Commonwealth Games, when India ended at a never-before fourth place on the medals table, jumping three places from the previous Games, winning sixty-nine medals overall. Thirty of those medals, five more than the total number of medals that India had won in the previous Games, were a bright, shining yellow. Remarkably, but perhaps not very surprisingly, more than half of those had been won by women.

Fifteen golds had been shared between shooters Anjali Bhagwat, Suma Shirur and Raj Kumari, and weightlifters Kunjarani Devi, Sanamacha Chanu, Pratima Kumari and Shailaja Pujari. But it was the sixteenth gold that was, in many ways, particularly special. In a Bollywood-style dream run, the unfancied Indian women's hockey team had manoeuvred its way past formidable Australia and England to claim the top prize. What made it poignant was that the team had been coached by Mir Ranjan Negi, the much-maligned goalie of the Indian men's hockey team that had lost the finals at the 1982 Asian Games to Pakistan, with a humiliating score of 1 goal to 7.

These were also the Games when Indian women gained podium finishes in new disciplines—Neelam Jaswant Singh scored a silver in the discus throw, Anju Bobby George won the long jump bronze, and Aparna Popat, won a bronze in badminton.

The Asian Games, held the same year, went well too, with Indian women burning up the track as they had been doing for a while at the Asiad—apart from the sprints and the middle-distance races, there were medals won at long jump, high jump, the heptathlon and the discus throw. But there was also something new, a sign of things to come, easily spotted in hindsight but perhaps not as evident then. In the tennis mixed doubles, Indian ace Leander Paes teamed up with a precocious fifteen-year-old from Hyderabad to win the bronze. Her name was Sania Mirza. The first of India's sporting 'daughters of liberalization' had entered the world stage and was already baring her very capable teeth.

On 14 November 2003, in an island tourist paradise in the Caribbean called Montego Bay, India's bid to host the Commonwealth Games at Delhi in 2010 won, beating out Canada's by a mile-wide margin. After failed bids to host the 1990 and 1994 Games, India had been acknowledged by the Commonwealth, if not yet as a sporting nation, at least as a country that wielded enough economic and political muscle to matter.

Athens 2004 came and went, leaving behind a flash of silver. Rajyavardhan Singh Rathore, who went on to become the minister for youth affairs and sports, followed up his brilliant gold-winning performance at the 2002 Commonwealth Games in the double trap shooting event (a feat he would repeat at the 2006 Games) with a silver-winning one at the Olympics, becoming the first Indian to win an Olympic silver in an individual event. There were also a couple of great women's stories on the sidelines—the women's 4x400-metre relay acquitted itself honourably, making the final again and finishing a very creditable seventh, and Anju Bobby George became the first Indian woman to make the final of an Olympic field event, finishing fifth in the world.

The 2006 Commonwealth Games were a bit of a downer, at least as far as the medal tally went. While India retained her No. 4 position on the medals table, the number of golds dropped to twenty-two. Among the women, the wrestlers, weightlifters and shooters gamely soldiered on, winning medals of all hues. The hockey team won again, a silver this time. And, as in every international competition since 2000, there was also something fresh to cheer about—new fronts had been thrown open, one in table tennis, where Indian women placed third in the team event, and the other in the discus throw, where Haryana's Seema Punia won the silver.

At the Asian Games the same year, chess wiz Humpy Koneru claimed gold in the women's rapid, and repeated the feat in the mixed team event. Sania, now twenty years old, became a role model for every Indian girl when she won gold in the mixed doubles and a silver each in the individual and team events. The women's 4x400-metre relay team, led by Manjeet Kaur, won gold. A twenty-four-year-old called Krishna Poonia (no relation to Seema) won the bronze in the discus throw. And the hockey team slipped a little, winning only a bronze.

That's right—*only* a bronze. Perhaps the biggest indicator of the change that was sweeping across Indian attitudes to winning at sport was this: six years into the new millennium, it was no longer politically incorrect to attach the word 'only' to a bronze medal won in a hockey tournament that included traditional heavyweights like Australia and England. In a sea change from Shiny Wilson's '[I] was not at all sad to lose the semi-final . . . qualifying itself was good enough for me',[4] the new breed of go-getter girls were given to excoriating themselves when they did not match up to their own expectations. Those expectations were always the same—to win, win, win.

The lifeblood of any sport, as everyone knows, is the fans. In this era of television-centric sports coverage, eyeballs (read: TRPs) are everything. It is viewership that brings in money, whether via tickets or telecast rights or sponsorship or merchandise, and it is money that is needed not only to keep the sport's reigning champions incentivized, but also to keep the sport itself relevant and attract new and exciting recruits. Cricket viewership had, of course, never been a problem in India, but with sporting success also coming from other fronts, and with the media's full support, other sports also gradually began to benefit. The one big challenge left was this—how to bring women, traditionally never big watchers of sport, into the fold?

Fortunately for all of us, Bollywood—specifically scriptwriter Jaideep Sahni—had seen the cinematic potential in the underdog story of the Indian women's hockey team, and their coach, way back in 2002. He wasted no time turning life into art, taking all the poetic licence required to adapt it for the screen. When it released in 2007, *Chak De! India* (Yash Raj Films)—based on a fictitious ragtag Indian women's hockey team that wins the 'World Championships'—became a watershed in the annals of Bollywood. Riding the country's optimistic mood, it used the attention that superstar Shah Rukh Khan garnered for it, not only to hold up a mirror to the deep-seated rot and sexism that plagued sports bodies, but also to dispense messages about courage, sportsmanship, teamwork, girl power, the reprehensibility of stereotyping, and the urban-rural and class divides. To keep things interesting, it also threw in snarky asides at the unofficial national sport, cricket.

With *Chak De!*'s success, the joy and grief of sport, its heady triumphs and its gutting defeats, and all the sacrifices it demanded of its practitioners became part of popular culture. The Indian sportswoman had been humanized, her peculiar trials—being a good daughter-in-law while trying to follow her dream, defying her parents and social expectations to travel to tournaments, being expected to let her achievements take a back seat to those of her fiancé's—showcased with a rare empathy. Across India, mothers and daughters—and fathers and sons—took the country's first contemporary sports film to their hearts.

The year after *Chak De!* brought women and girls out into movie halls and into sporting goods stores (there was a serious spike in the sales of hockey sticks nationwide, and most of the buyers were girls), cricket itself, willy-nilly, helped the cause along, with the introduction of the forty-five-day annual family carnival called the Indian Premier League (IPL). Social media, which had recently exploded on the scene, helped things along. Going to a sports stadium was no longer something that only the serious sports fans and stats nerds did—it had become a selfie-worthy social occasion, a community celebration. Single-handedly, the IPL changed the demographic of your fellow sports-watcher—he was now your wife.

~

The 2008 Summer Olympics at Beijing will always have a very special place in Indian sporting history. It was at these Games that the twenty-five-year-old shooter, Abhinav Bindra, already one of the best in the world in his category (in the qualifying rounds at Athens in 2004, he had broken the Olympic record but still lost out on a medal; and he had won India's first-ever shooting gold at the World Championships in 2006), finally fulfilled his Olympic destiny, winning for his country its very first gold in an individual event, ever. But there was more to celebrate—wrestler Sushil Kumar won a bronze in his category, and so did boxer Vijender Singh, bringing up the country's medal tally to three, a never-before event. Among the other eye-catchers was badminton star Saina Nehwal, only eighteen, who became the first Indian woman to reach the quarter-finals of her event in the Olympics.

This outcome was unexpected, and gratefully embraced by a nation that had suffered heartache and humiliation in the lead-up to Beijing—the men's hockey team, which had won no less than eight golds, two silvers and one bronze in its glittering history at the Olympics since 1928, had failed to qualify, and the women weightlifters, dogged by doping allegations for the last several years, had been banned from the Games, muddying the legacy of Karnam Malleswari.

But there was no time to dwell on either the highs or the lows of 2008, for India was readying for its most ambitious international sports challenge to date—the hosting of the Commonwealth Games 2010. With infrastructure projects already hugely delayed and political discourse descending into the familiar morass of allegations and counter-allegations of corruption, misuse of power, budget overruns and unfulfilled promises, the dark cloud of self-doubt and despondency about our lack of integrity as a nation, never too far away, was back to haunt us, hovering over dinner-table conversations, fed by the media narrative. As the Games drew closer and it seemed as if we were destined to fail spectacularly, reversing all the hard-won gains to our reputation over the two decades since liberalization, top athletes began to pull out of the Games, citing reasons as varied as possible terrorist attacks, monsoon floods and lack of hygiene at the Games Village.

But in the *akhara*s and archery academies, the running tracks and shooting ranges, the badminton and table-tennis courts and hockey stadiums across India, many of them now supported by generous inflows of corporate and government money, the mood was upbeat. In these hallowed places, acutely conscious that the home advantage that was theirs in these Games would not return for several years, the first wave of the daughters of liberalization were hitting their stride, getting ready to take their game out of Asia and on to the world stage, and win.

And did they win! For the first time in the history of the Commonwealth Games, and supported by thousands of fans who thronged the stadiums to support their boys and girls, India ended an unprecedented second on the medals table, yards behind behemoth Australia but ahead of England and Canada, winning over 100 medals. And while the men won many more medals overall than the women, it was the latter who were breaching long-standing barriers—Krishna Poonia became the first Indian woman to win a Commonwealth gold in athletics when she hurled the discus farther than anyone else in the field, Geeta Phogat became the first Indian woman wrestler to win a gold, and Kavita Raut (now Tungar) the first woman to win an individual track medal when she won a bronze in the 10,000 metres.

The roster of the other medal winners in the women's events was long and impressive, but the real breakthrough was in the number of different disciplines that women were now winning at. As each day passed and more Indian medals were rung up on the leader board, the country's sporting intelligence and engagement soared. More and more Indians began to tune in to the Games, acquainting themselves with the rules of competition in events that they had had no previous familiarity with—recurve archery, for one. These were the Games when recurve archers Deepika Kumari (two golds), Dola Banerjee (one gold and one bronze) and Bombayla Devi (one gold), and shooters Anisa Sayyed (two golds), Rahi Sarnobat (one gold and one silver) and Heena Sidhu (one gold and one silver) became household names, as did Jwala Gutta and Ashwini Ponnappa (gold, women's doubles, badminton). Sania (silver) and Saina (gold) continued to dominate their sports.

The momentum of the Commonwealth Games in October carried over to the Asian Games the very next month—India put on a fine showing, winning a total of sixty-five medals, including fourteen golds. Among the women who won gold medals were a few new names—Preeja Sreedharan (10,000 metres), Sudha Singh (3000-metre steeplechase) and Ashwini Akkunji (400-metre hurdles).

It was also during the 2010 Asian Games that we first heard the name of a sport called wushu, aka Chinese kung fu, a full-contact martial art. Notwithstanding our ignorance, some of our girls were apparently already pretty good at it—for Sandhyarani Devi Wangkhem of Manipur won herself India's first wushu silver! It was things like this—a silver medal for an Indian woman at an unknown sport in an international competition—that really signalled that things were getting better and better for Indian sport in general, and for Indian sportswomen in particular.

Plus, there were the sports whose larger stages lay outside the ambit of the Olympics, the Asian Games and the Commonwealth Games—sports like tennis, badminton, boxing, cricket and chess. And our girls were doing marvellously there as well.

By 2010, gutsy Sania had shrugged off a fatwa issued against her for the length of her skirts and a legal case against her ostensible disrespect for the national flag and soared through to the World Top 30 in singles tennis rankings. At the Australian Open in 2006, she became the first Indian woman to be seeded in a Grand Slam event. By 2010, Saina, she of the multicoloured hair clips, had become the first Indian, male or female, to win a BWF Superseries title, one of the Holy Grails in badminton, and was ruling the roost as World No. 2.

By 2010, Magnificent Mary Kom, the gritty boxer from Manipur, had already won the World Amateur Boxing Championships no less than five times! No other Indian, man or woman, had come close to achieving anything like it. By 2010, Mithali Raj, the highest run-scorer in women's international cricket and one of the greatest women to wield a cricket bat, had led India to a thrilling World Cup final.

By 2010, Koneru Humpy, still only twenty-three, had been a grandmaster for eight years. In 2007, she became only the second woman, after Judith Polgar, to exceed the 2600 Elo rating. By 2010, Tania Sachdev had been grandmaster for five years, and won the Asian Chess Championship.

For the first time since I had become a fan, it was becoming extraordinarily difficult to keep up with all the good stuff that was going on. If ever there was a time when young India was spoilt for choice when it came to picking and choosing its female sporting role models, this was it. That was why, like hundreds of other families from across the country, my husband and I travelled to Delhi during the Commonwealth Games, with our thirteen-year-old daughter and eight-year-old son in tow. We wanted them to see, first-hand, the world-beating grit of their compatriots on display, hear the gladiatorial roar of the crowd as one of ours crossed the finish line ahead of the others, experience the heart-swelling emotion that comes with hearing the national anthem play as a champion wearing Indian colours mounts the top step of the podium. Like tens of thousands of other children—and adults!—they came away inspired, their attitude towards their country tweaked in a small, difficult-to-articulate but utterly irrevocable way.

~

Before we knew it, it was 2012, and time for the London Olympics. Excitement was running high, and India obliged, ending those Games with six medals, twice the number it had won at any other Olympics, ever. Of the four bronzes in the kitty, two had the names of women—Mary Kom and Saina Nehwal. There were other noteworthy achievements—Krishna Poonia entered the last eight in the discus throw, and finished sixth, and Usha protégée Tintu Luka made it to the semi-final stage of the 800 metres.

The 2014 Commonwealth Games, expectedly, was a bit of a crash-landing after the high of Delhi 2010—sixty-four total medals as against 101, of which only fifteen were gold. As always, though, there was enough to cheer about, for the Games ushered in the next generation of female sporting rock stars. Among the golds were weightlifter Sanjita Chanu, wrestlers Babita Kumari Phogat and Vinesh Phogat (who are cousins; Babita's sister, Geeta, had won the gold at the previous Games), and squash champs Joshna Chinappa and Dipika Pallikal; among the silvers, weightlifter Mirabai Chanu and wrestler Sakshi Malik; among the bronzes, 'giant killer' boxer Pinki Rani Jangra, who had knocked out world champ Mary Kom in the qualification trials, badminton star P.V. Sindhu, and, for the first time ever, an Indian woman gymnast, nineteen-year-old Dipa Karmakar.

But Indian sportspeople, sports fans, legal eagles, gender activists and anyone who believes strongly in fairness and gender equality both on and off the sports field will remember the 2014 Commonwealth Games as a landmark for quite another reason. That was the year eighteen-year-old national sprint champion Dutee Chand, who had just won golds at the Asian Junior Championships in both the 200 metres and the 4x400-metre relay, becoming the first Indian athlete to do so, was informed that she would not be allowed to compete against other women athletes at Glasgow because her testosterone levels exceeded the permissible limits for a woman, as laid down by the IAAF. High levels of testosterone were believed to help build muscle and make athletes faster, thus conferring a biological advantage on a woman who had more than her 'fair share'.

Dutee was stunned. Her high testosterone levels were not only entirely natural but surprisingly common, a by-product of a condition called polycystic ovary syndrome, which afflicts one in seven young women in any population. Furious at her exclusion and humiliated by the insinuation that she was 'almost a man', she decided to drag the IAAF to court to challenge its 'permissible levels' of the offending hormone. If Michael Phelps's freakishly wide wingspan and Usain Bolt's never-ending legs were not considered 'biological advantages', how come her own medical condition was? In fact, there was no real data on just how much of an advantage an athlete gained merely by having high levels of testosterone—many experts had dismissed the IAAF's claims as 'bad science'.

India's sports ministry, the Sports Authority of India, and some of our best lawyers and activists rallied around Dutee. International experts were brought in, and a Canadian law firm agreed to take on the case pro bono.

On 25 July 2015, in a landmark judgement, the Court of Arbitration for Sport overturned Dutee's ban—and the bans against every other female athlete in the world who had been similarly discriminated against—and ruled that the ceiling on testosterone levels would be suspended for two years, while the IAAF gathered proof to support their assertions of testosterone-linked biological advantage. An Indian woman's unwillingness to back down in the face of an unjust rule had resulted in a fairer world, if not for everyone, at least for some sportswomen.

In 2016, twenty-year-old Dutee qualified for the 100-metre sprint at the Rio Olympics. No other Indian woman had qualified for that particular event before or after Usha, who had achieved the feat at the Moscow Olympics in 1980, sixteen years before Dutee was born.

But we've gotten ahead of ourselves. Let's go back to 2014, and to the Incheon Asian Games, which arrived right on the heels of Glasgow. India ended at eighth place, two places down from the previous Games, but women were among the medals, as always. Among them were M.C. Mary Kom, Sania Mirza and Seema Punia, who won gold (as did the 4x400-metre relay team and the kabaddi team); Tintu Luka, who won silver (as did the squash team); and Vinesh Phogat, Dipika Pallikal, sprinter M.R. Poovamma and steeplechaser Lalita Babar, who won bronze. But perhaps the most cheering thing about Incheon 2014 was the resurgence of the Indian women's hockey team under Ritu Rani, a fine halfback who had debuted for India at Doha 2006, at the tender age of fourteen. At Incheon, she led her team back to the podium for the first time in twelve years—they finished with a bronze.

~

Who were these girls with the winning ways? Where had they come from? What inspired them to keep going? In sport, as in everything else in life, the truth is to be found not on the podium, but in the backstory. The fascinating thing is that each backstory is quite unlike any other—the nudge that first pitches a girl into a particular sport; the insanely difficult journey to the top, as much a test of her mental and emotional strength as her physical; the kind of social, economic and cultural background she comes from, which helps or hinders her progress in particular ways— the factors are specific to each person; they can never be whittled down to four or five neat categories.

Even more fascinating, however, are the unexpected fallouts of such success, especially in terms of its social and cultural impact. Mary Kom moved from athletics to boxing at the age of seventeen because she was inspired by the medal-winning success of her fellow Manipuri, Dingko Singh, at the Bangkok Asiad in 1998. She didn't tell her dad about it because she knew he would not allow it—he worried too much, as dads of daughters did, about the damage boxing could do to her face and how that might affect her chances in the marriage market. Her stupendous success has not only brought a slew of exceptional sportspeople from the region on to the national stage, it has led to an increased awareness about, and respect for, her state in national consciousness. In its turn, the eponymous Bollywood movie made on her life has hopefully inspired a generation of young women—and more importantly, young men—to rethink their notions of what a supportive husband really means.

Geeta and Babita took to wrestling not because of any love for the sport, but because their wrestler dad insisted they did. After waiting several years in vain for a son, Mahavir Singh Phogat decided he would coach his daughters to be wrestlers instead, and brave the social backlash that would undoubtedly accompany such an act in his conservative town. Today, the success of his audacious experiment—which, it must be said, could have gone very badly for him and his girls—has not only propelled many more girls from Haryana into wrestling and other sports, but has also brought about a sea change in the mindset of a patriarchal state that had the worst sex ratio at birth among all states in India as per the 2011 census: 834 girls to every 1000 boys. In early 2018, the ratio had gone up a remarkable 80 points to 914, and one cannot help but wonder how much of the credit for this should go to an iconoclast called Mahavir Phogat, whose experiment is captured in the blockbuster movie, *Dangal* (2016, Aamir Khan Productions, UTV Motion Pictures, Walt Disney Pictures India).

Saina (who, like the Phogat sisters, was another Haryana girl responsible for altering perspectives about women in her home state) and Sindhu owe their success, in large part, to their extraordinary coach, Pullela Gopichand, who mortgaged his own home in 2008 to pull together the final tranche of funds needed to complete his state-of-the-art facility in Hyderabad, the Gopichand Badminton Academy, where the two girls now train. Today, the academy counts among its students the recent World No. 1s in both the men's and the women's games. More importantly, Gopi has set the standard for other centres of sporting excellence around the country, and proved that 'world-class' is an adjective that can now be legitimately attached to an Indian sporting academy.

Star forward of the women's hockey team, Rani Rampal (also from Haryana), was only fifteen when she smashed home four goals against Belgium in the Champions Challenge Hockey Tournament in 2009, helping India to a 6-3 win and winning herself the Best Young Player title. When I interviewed her for a story on teen achievers for a children's magazine the same year, she sounded very excited about life, particularly because of a monthly grant of Rs 4000 that she had begun to receive from a young Bengaluru-based non-profit, GoSports Foundation. 'I can now buy better shoes and kit to improve my game,'[5] she told me, grinning widely. 'My father is a cart-puller, so there has never been money to spare for such luxuries.' Four thousand rupees may not seem like a lot of money at all, but that small infusion, made at the appropriate time, had made all the difference to a budding hockey superstar and her family—it had allowed her to chase her dream without guilt. Across India, other organizations such as GoSports, although they were few and far between, were making that happen for other young and hungry sportspeople.

From sprawling metropolises and remote villages, from straitened circumstances and comfortable ones, from families with no background in sport and families that had fine sporting pedigrees—by 2014, the sporting valiants who were busting society's notions of what a girl wanted, and giving the Indian public a masterclass in single-minded determination, were coming from everywhere. The incentives were different—success, respect in society, financial independence, a means to negotiate life on their own terms—but the goal was the same: to win. The support system was falling in place too. The idea of women in sport—whether as sportspeople, journalists, supportive mums, or fans—had truly begun to gather mass appeal.

~

Rio 2016. Anticipation was at fever pitch as India sent her largest contingent ever—117 athletes—to the Olympics. Unlike in the earlier Games, the 117 were fairly evenly split between male and female athletes—sixty-three men to fifty-four women. India came back with only two medals—both, it has to be mentioned, won by women—but it is the 130 per cent spike in the numbers of the female athletes, from twenty-three in London to a gobsmacking fifty-four in Rio (the number of male athletes had only gone up from sixty to sixty-three), that tells the real story. For the first time since 1980, Ritu Rani's girls—the women's hockey team—had qualified for the Olympics, adding a healthy sixteen to the contingent. And a much higher number of athletes than usual had earned the right, with spectacular timings, distances and performances, to stand up and be counted among the greatest in the world.

The ones who achieved the greatest sporting distinction of all—an Olympic medal—were Sindhu, who became the first Indian woman to win a silver at the Olympics (it could so easily have been a gold, but doughty Carolina Marin had the measure of our Sindhu on the day), and wrestler Sakshi, who won the wrestling bronze in the 58-kg category. But the girl who won the most hearts with her bravura performance a few minutes before midnight on the eve of India's seventieth Independence Day, when she leapt off the vaulting horse in a dangerous double-somersault, was Tripura's Dipa Karmakar. Dipa missed the bronze by a whisker, but her countrymen, who had stayed up to watch her, weren't complaining.

Dipa and her coach, Bisweswar Nandi, did not know that, however. 'After she finished fourth,' recounted Nandi in an interview just after they had returned, 'I was so terrified to think of the backlash in India.' So was Dipa. 'Sir,' she told Nandi, 'when we land [they were scheduled to arrive in New Delhi at 3.30 a.m.], we will quietly hire an auto and go straight to IG Stadium. Nobody will notice.' Nandi agreed.[6]

No one can say which of the two was more stunned when they emerged from the airport terminal. Waiting in the predawn darkness were crowds of fans who erupted into cheers the moment they caught sight of their young heroine. 'I never thought that there would be people at the airport to receive me,' said an emotional Dipa later. '*Mujhe toh laga tha ki koi nahi aayega kyunki medal toh jeeta nahi maine.*'[7]

That little story illustrates another huge change in the Indian sports fan's attitude to her team's performance—like her country, the sports fan was now mature and confident enough in her own skin to appreciate the achievement, not just the win. Her outlook was broader too—she did not line the streets only to greet the cricket team when they won the World Cup, she also turned up at the airport to sneak a peek at the girl who was the fourth-best gymnast in the world.

The other thing that happened at Rio was that golf was reinstated as an Olympic sport. That in itself was not particularly exciting; what was, was that Indian teenager Aditi Ashok almost made the podium! Astounding things like that had now become par for the course in Indian sport.

Right after the Summer Olympics came the Rio Paralympics, and another huge win. For the first time, India, which had sent its largest contingent of nineteen, won four medals—more than what our 117-strong contingent had won at the regular Olympics—at the Paralympics, *two* of them gold. Which was incredible, but what gave fans of women in sport even more to cheer about was the lone silver won by Deepa Malik, who hurled the shot-put to a distance of 4.61 metres from her wheelchair, making her the first Indian woman Paralympic athlete to win a medal.

And so, two years later, to the Commonwealth Games of 2018. With a fabulous haul of twenty-six golds, India jumped two spots to end up at number three on the medals table, her best standing since Delhi 2010. Among the golds were a bunch of female shooters, including usual suspects (it must be said, it gives me serious goosebumps to use those words so casually) Tejaswini Sawant, twice gold-medal winner at the Commonwealth Games of 2006, and Heena Sidhu.

Oh, also, Mary Kom, Saina Nehwal, and Vinesh Phogat did their thing, all of them ending up with golds. Ho-hum.

But while 'been there, done that' had actually become a thing with some of our fine ladies, what was truly thrilling was to see a young guard emerge to carry on the fine work of their seniors. Young shooter Manu Bhaker, sixteen, won gold, while her teammate, Mehuli Ghosh, seventeen, won silver. Twenty-two-year-old paddler Manika Batra led the table tennis team to gold, while also winning the individual gold in the singles and a silver in the doubles. And an eighteen-year-old from Assam called Hima Das not only made it to the last eight in the 400 metres, but also finished a very creditable sixth.

The writing was on the wall—the sporting success of India's girls wasn't a flash in the pan. The village was in place, the juggernaut was on the move. Unless something went horribly wrong, our girls would only go from strength to strength. It was the kind of message that was entirely designed to warm the cockles of a long-time fan's heart.

~

12 July 2018, almost thirty-five years to the day after Usha missed her chance of becoming India's first Olympic medallist in a track event. The summer skies over the

Ratina Stadium in Tampere, Finland, venue of the IAAF Under-20 World Athletics Championships, are still bright at 8.10 p.m., the scheduled time for the start of the women's 400-metre final. Running in Lane 4 is Indian sprinter Hima Das, still eighteen, the fastest qualifier in the field with a timing of 52:10 in the semis. It is far, far short of her personal best of 51:13, and everyone, including the commentators, knows this well. 'Has Das's moment come?' wonders one of them. 'Has India's moment come in global track athletics?' It's all a little surreal—for both fans and other sportspersons, past and present—to know that an Indian girl is the 'clear favourite' to win an international track event.

The finalists take their positions at the starting blocks and are about to take off when they are asked to stand up again—the photographers are too close to the tracks and have to be moved away. The tension is palpable. The girls fidget, stretching, warming up once more, restless. Soon enough, they are at the blocks again, and this time, they're off like streaks of lightning the moment they hear the starter's gun. As the 100- and 200-metre marks are passed and Hima is not even among the top four, a deep sense of déjà vu grips the Indians who are watching—will this race end like that other one did, all those years ago?

The runners enter the last straight. The race is almost done. Hima is moving faster now, looking stronger, but is it too little, too late?

And then, suddenly, magically, miraculously, goosebump-inducingly, *incredibly*, Hima Das begins to fly. One by one, she passes the athletes ahead of her, and then pulls away cleanly, crossing the finish line at 51.46, ahead of the rest not by a whisker, not by a nose, but by absolute *yards*, winning India her first-ever track gold at a world-level athletics event. The jinx has been broken, the ghosts of 1960 and 1984 have finally been laid to rest.

To my great regret, I was fast asleep when this race was run. But I needn't have worried about missing it. The next morning, I discovered that the million different factions of my country, and the many different worlds I myself inhabit, had coalesced in the night. In the ultimate modern-day expression of unity in diversity, the video clip of Hima winning was being furiously forwarded on every single WhatsApp group—family, school moms, work colleagues, college classmates—that I was part of.

To most people, the sight of our strong, brave girl letting her tears flow on the podium as the national anthem played was the most moving part of her win. If I had to pick my own heart-swelling rah-rah moment, though, I would pick the one that came right after the race, when Hima, straight-backed and smiling, not winded in the least after that dream run, strutted around the unfamiliar foreign stadium like she owned it, pumping her arms in the air, urging everyone there to acknowledge and cheer her win, sending out a strong message—*Get used to world-beating brown girls*!

~

Depending on what scale you are using, thirty-five years—1984 to 2019—is a lifetime, or the blink of an eye.

In an ancient and ridiculously diverse country of well over a billion people, where change comes at an agonizingly slow pace because every adult has a vote and an opinion, thirty-four years is not a long time at all, only half the number of years since we won our freedom from almost two centuries of a crippling foreign rule that destroyed our confidence and well-nigh broke our spirit.

In thirty-five years, we have gone from being, in our own eyes, a country of losers, to a country where anything, even something as surreal as world-domination in sport—which, if you take away the bells and whistles, is no more than an indulgence, a non-essential appendix to the hardcore business of life—cannot entirely be ruled out, at least in our minds. Who can argue with the assertion that in addition to everything else, it is our gallant, winning sportswomen who have contributed, in no small measure, to this incredible, and incredibly rapid, transformation?

Do I, then, wish I could be a thirteen-year-old sports fan in 2018, rather than in 1984? Do I wish I could have grown up in a country where girls took the notion of Indian women winning at sport for granted, who did not berate themselves for not knowing the name of a particular world-beating diva because, seriously, there were so many of them, and who considered a career in sport—not as a sportsperson necessarily, but in some related area—because that was something that people routinely did?

Nah. For the thirty-five-year-long ride, with all its ups and ups, has been exhilarating. I wouldn't have missed it for the world.

Deepthi Bopaiah, formerly a wealth adviser and a trainer during her stint of six years with HSBC, joined GoSports Foundation in 2012 after deciding to pursue a long-standing interest in sport. A sportswoman herself, she has previously represented her university and Karnataka state in tennis and basketball. Deepthi holds a business degree in finance and marketing from Symbiosis, Pune, and has a master's degree in economics from Pune University.

The Alchemist

While the men's hockey team had won the Olympic gold on eight previous occasions, the Indian contingent departed for the 2008 Olympic Games with the knowledge that no Indian individual had ever achieved the feat. On 11 August 2008 in Beijing, with a masterful performance in the 10-metre air rifle event, Abhinav Bindra definitively answered the long-standing question—is an Indian capable of winning an individual Olympic gold? Bindra's achievement has given Indian athletes the belief that they are capable of winning on the biggest stages in world sport.

Abhinav Bindra on the Olympic podium

Courtesy: Heinz Reinkemeier

India's only individual
Olympic gold medal

Courtesy: Abhinav Bindra

The Big League

In the backdrop of India's win in the inaugural ICC World Twenty20 in 2007, the Indian Premier League was launched by the BCCI in 2008. The IPL brought together a heady cocktail of cricket and entertainment, attracted new audiences and introduced private investment and participation to Indian cricket.

Courtesy: BCCI

The IPL pits India teammates like *M.S. Dhoni* and *Virat Kohli* against each other

Courtesy: BCCI

Indian and international cricketers go under the hammer during the IPL Auction each year and earn unprecedented sums

The Big League

The franchise-based league has since set new benchmarks for event management, player compensation, viewership, broadcasting, media rights and brand value in cricket. Now, the best cricketers in the world aspire to make a career playing in the IPL, a far cry from previous decades when many international players toured India with reluctance.

Courtesy: BCCI

Ricky Ponting and *Sachin Tendulkar* combine routines as they open the batting together

Courtesy: BCCI

The IPL breathed new life into the careers of cricketers like West Indian batsman *Chris Gayle*

Multisport Nation

The 1983 World Cup victory wove cricket into the national fabric. The massive fan following and commercial success it has enjoyed has often been blamed for the neglect of other sports in India.

The *Indian national football team*, known as the 'Blue Tigers', has a passionate and growing legion of supporters

Viswanathan Anand was India's first chess grandmaster and a *World Chess Champion*

Multisport Nation

Over the last decade, Indian athletes have produced world-class performances in a wide range of disciplines, first in a trickle, then in a steady stream. Boxers, badminton players, wrestlers and gymnasts have become household names, the subjects of popular feature films and books and brand endorsements. Cricket might still be the most popular sport by some distance, but India can be called a 'one-sport nation' no more.

Pankaj Advani has won the *World Championships* in billiards and snooker twenty-one times

Sakshi Malik won a bronze medal in wrestling at the *2016 Rio Olympics*

Net Benefit

In 1980, Prakash Padukone won the prestigious All England Open. Pullela Gopichand repeated this achievement in 2001. This was not the last we would hear of these badminton champions. Upon retirement, both turned coaches and set up eponymous badminton coaching academies, which have bred a host of senior and junior players of repute.

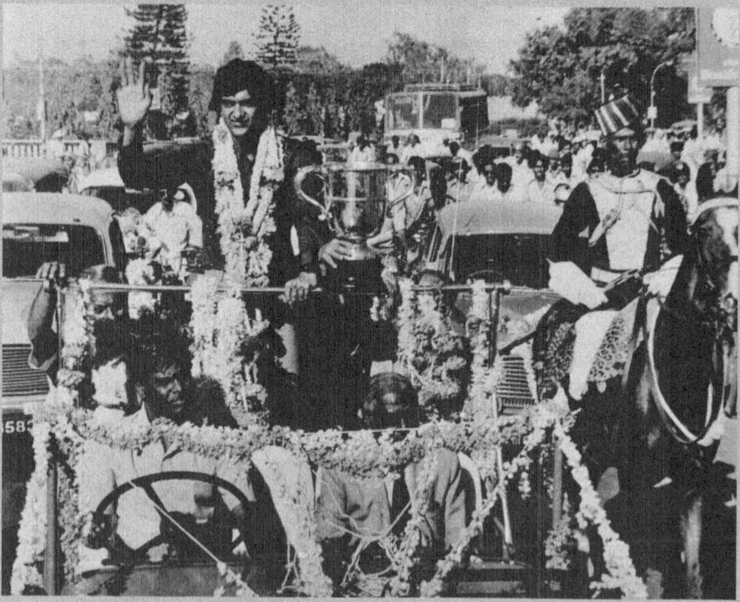

Courtesy; Prakash Padukone

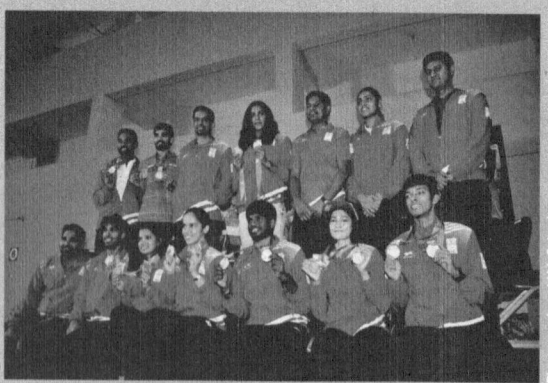

Prakash Padukone is feted on his return home after his ***All England triumph***

Photographer: V.V. Subrahmanyam

The ***Indian badminton team***, winners of a historic ***2018 Commonwealth Games gold***, pose with Pullela Gopichand (standing, third from left)

Net Benefit

Saina Nehwal and Kidambi Srikanth have gone on to hold the World No. 1 singles ranking, Nehwal and P.V. Sindhu clinched Olympic medals and H.S. Prannoy and Lakshya Sen have each won a Youth Olympics medal. In a reversal of trends, Indians are now the ones whom opponents would prefer not to face in their part of the draw.

Saina Nehwal won an Olympic bronze medal at the *London 2012 Olympics* and rose to the *World No. 1* spot in the badminton rankings

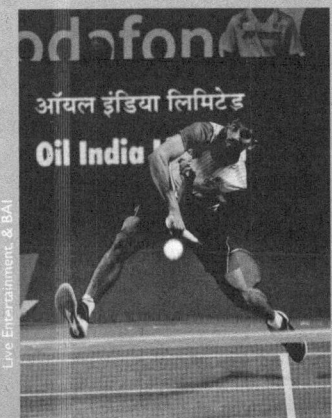

Kidambi Srikanth became the first male *World No. 1* shuttler from India in the modern ranking era

The Wonder Women

Some saw a glass ceiling, others broke through it to find what was above. Despite facing numerous societal and practical challenges and inequities, India's women athletes have been at the forefront of the sporting movement. They repeatedly outshine their male counterparts, and have steadily increased their prominence and numbers in Indian contingents at major international events.

Courtesy: PBL, Sportz & Live Entertainment, & BAI

P.V. Sindhu won silver medals at the ***2016 Rio Olympics*** and the ***World Badminton Championships*** in 2017 and 2018, and won the 2018 World Tour Finals

Photographer: Bhavesh Bhati

Dipa Karmakar became India's first-ever female Olympic gymnast at *Rio 2016*, finishing fourth in the vault

The Wonder Women

This progress has also helped shine the spotlight on the achievements of and talent in national teams, the women's cricket team being a case in point. Along the way, India's women achievers have begun changing beliefs, perceptions and outcomes, both on and off the field.

M.C. Mary Kom, six-time *World Boxing Champion*, trains wards at her academy in Imphal

The *Indian women's cricket team* finished runners-up at the *ICC Women's World Cup in 2017*

No-Hyphens

Despite a fair degree of success at international competitions over the years, Indian disability sport was minimally supported and covered and was largely off the national radar. India's haul of four Paralympic medals in Rio 2016, including two gold medals, was juxtaposed with the disappointing haul of two medals at the corresponding Olympics.

Copyright: GoSports Foundation

Murlikant Petkar, with a historic performance in the swimming event at the *1972 Paralympics in Heidelberg,* won India's first Paralympic gold medal

Photographer: Bhavesh Bhati

Devendra Jhajharia is a two-time *Paralympic gold medallist* in javelin F46, winning medals at Athens 2004 and Rio 2016

No-Hyphens

With a little help from various quarters, the movement came to life in an unprecedented way, with India enveloping, celebrating and rewarding her Para athletes on a par with their able-bodied counterparts. Significant gains have since been made by Indian athletes at international competitions such as the Asian Para Games. While much work remains to be done to promote disability sport, there is a palpable sense of possibility and hope that sport can create better lives for India's vast differently abled population.

Photographer: Bhavesh Bhati

Deepa Malik became the first Indian woman to win a *Paralympic medal* when she won silver in shot-put at Rio 2016

Photographer: Dilpreet Sandhu

Suyash Jadhav won India's first-ever gold medal in swimming at the *Asian Para Games 2018*

Governing the Governors

Historically, Indian sports administration has been dogged by inefficiency and lack of transparency. Given the political entrenchment in a number of sports bodies, the status quo has been difficult to alter. The legal framework has struggled to balance the 'autonomy' of sports bodies with their public accountability.

The *Indian sports administration* is gradually waking up to the need to remove unnecessary obstacles in athletes' paths

The National Games, India's premier national-level multisport event, has been the subject of delays and postponements on a number of occasions

Caps on age and tenure have ended the reigns of several veteran sports administrators

Governing the Governors

This state of play continued until the judiciary found it fit to intervene. In a series of cases involving the most prominent sports bodies in India, the Supreme Court of India and various high courts have carved out various principles of good governance and imposed them on these bodies. While it remains to be seen whether these principles become ubiquitous and improve governance performance across the board, the needle of accountability has moved forward in several irreversible ways.

REPORT

OF

THE SUPREME COURT COMMITTEE

ON

REFORMS IN CRICKET

The *Justice R.M. Lodha Committee report* recommending reforms in cricket governance was adopted almost in its entirety by the Supreme Court in a landmark judgment

The Professionals

With relatively empty event calendars, rudimentary administration and heavy reliance on government funding being the norm, the success of the IPL gave hope to many—of financial opportunity to other federations, entrepreneurial reward to private stakeholders and new career opportunities to Indian and international athletes. Private franchise-based leagues, sanctioned by federations, have been launched in a wide variety of disciplines. Name a sport and it either has or is probably contemplating a professional league.

The *Indian Super League* is an ambitious project that has steadily grown in popularity since its first season in 2014

Carolina Marin, Olympic champion and former World No. 1, has turned up regularly in the *Premier Badminton League* along with a host of international badminton stars

The Professionals

The Pro Kabaddi League, which repackaged a popular indigenous sport, has been the most popular of these. Leagues have also been promoted in football, badminton, tennis, hockey, wrestling, cue sports, table tennis and volleyball, among others. These leagues are certainly not the panacea for all the ills prevalent in Indian sport, and many have failed to build sustainable business models. However, they have brought a previously unseen degree of professionalism to sports management and have enabled careers for athletes on the field and for managers off it.

The *Pro Kabaddi League* has brought professionalism and a new profile to a traditional Indian sport

The *Pro Volleyball League* had its inaugural season in 2019 and has shown early promise

Generation Next

One of Indian sport's strangest paradoxes was that financial support and backing usually came only to those who had already achieved significant success. This begged the question of what resources—besides a hope and a prayer—were available to achieve success in the first place. With bigger public budgets for sport, changing government support structures and the introduction of corporate social responsibility laws encouraging private investments in talent development, new avenues and pathways have opened for emerging athletes as they navigate their transitions to senior competition. The next generation of Indian athletes has a new DNA—of fearlessness, aspiration, confidence and a genuine belief that they belong among the best in the world.

Jeremy Lalrinnunga became the first Indian to win a Youth Olympics gold medal with his weightlifting triumph in 2018

Hima Das won gold in the 400 metres at the World U-20 Championships 2018

Lakshya Sen won silver in badminton at the 2018 Youth Olympics

Neeraj Chopra won gold and broke the world record in javelin at the U-20 World Junior Championships in 2016

8

The Indian Paralympic
Story Comes of Age

Deepthi Bopaiah and Aparna Ravichandran

India's first individual gold on the biggest stage in world sport. You may be thinking of Abhinav Bindra's Olympic medal in 2008, but our first individual gold actually came way back in Heidelberg, Germany, at the 1972 Paralympics.

Murlikant Petkar, an army jawan at EME Secunderabad, took to international sport like a duck to water. A boxing enthusiast and javelin ace, he took seven bullets to his spine during the 1965 India-Pakistan war. Five years later, he made the rare and privileged discovery that his international gold medal at the 1970 Commonwealth Games resulted in the national flag being raised in his honour. In 1972, at his debut Paralympics in Heidelberg, not knowing the local language and still adapting to foreign food, he broke the world record for 50-metre freestyle swimming in his event.

What pushed this simple yet outrageously talented village boy towards global excellence? The doctor who recommended swimming for rehabilitation to the wounded soldier, the eagle eye of a coach who spotted his innate swimming talent and the support of a few strategic well-wishers along the way, including his employers, led by the illustrious J.R.D. Tata.

This medal came twenty-five years after India attained Independence, and for various reasons, has not become part of popular Indian sporting lore. One can only hypothesize that our society was perhaps too preoccupied at the time with other aspects of nation-building. Sport—especially Para sport—did not grab the common man's imagination, perhaps because the story was not told in Technicolor detail at the time. This was a missed opportunity to rebuild a nation that was dealing with the aftermath of two wars by celebrating a home-grown champion who had won on the biggest stage of all.

The Para sport movement has stood neglected and largely undeveloped in India over the years. One may even wonder why we need a separate Paralympic Games when we have the Olympic Games, which functions as the biggest carnival of world sport. Why can't the Olympic Games incorporate Para events, as the Commonwealth Games does? There is a straightforward, simple and pragmatic response to that—to give differently abled athletes a *parallel* stage of their own, one that does not have its roots in sympathy, or the dialectic between ability and disability. Having had the good fortune to witness the Paralympics and Asian Para Games, we staunchly support having separate events, given how the competing athletes stand apart and distinguish themselves, not simply for the physical reasons one would imagine.

The story of another such medallist from Punjab is as wondrous as that of Murlikant. In the late 1970s, in a village named Mehsampur in Punjab, Rajinder Rahelu was born with poliomyelitis. Oblivious to the concept of a wheelchair, unable to recognize the requirements of his physical challenge, Rajinder performed his own chores by crawling from one room to the other as a boy.

Gifted with a powerful upper body honed by having to compensate for his stunted lower body, Rajinder was pushed in the direction of bench-press events and grew up competing with able-bodied athletes. As late as 2002, he was still far from aiming to compete at the Paralympics. He only heard about his current event, powerlifting, for the first time when the chairman of Powerlifting India, Vijay B. Munishwar, laid eyes on him and subsequently pushed him to make the switch to the discipline. Far from being inspired, Rajinder had to overcome an initial resistance to the idea of competing with other 'disabled' people. Then again, why wouldn't he? After all, he had grown up competing with able-bodied athletes as their equal. In India, then as it is now, admitting to a disability almost inevitably elicited feelings of pity and placed you in a position of helplessness and dependence.

Rajinder had always taken charge of his life. Not one to be daunted by the prospect of travel for competition, he had even changed trains without a wheelchair on his way to one of the Nationals. For anyone familiar with the chaos and hubbub of Indian train stations, it is incredible to picture the sight and self-confidence of this youngster, believing that he could crawl from one platform to the other without injury. Unfortunately, he did get injured. He eventually found out about wheelchairs, but the cost of one was absolutely prohibitive to him. Since there was no way he could spend Rs 5000–6000 on such 'luxury', he fashioned one for himself! Well-meaning friends helped him with ideas as well as the product design. Rajinder eventually ended up using the wheelchair from 1999 right up until the Athens Paralympics in 2004, where he won the bronze medal in powerlifting.

What drives a person to compete in sport, in a seemingly thankless profession devoid of the prospect of reward or recognition? Murlikant had attempted to fight for national honours and government rewards post his Paralympic medal, but soon gave up the quest. Rajinder had never even heard of the Arjuna Award when he was informed that he was in line to win it—as a result of his Athens Paralympic medal! While the Arjuna Award came to him relatively easily, he then had to embark on a six-year chase, along with Devendra Jhajharia, the javelin-throwing gold medallist from the 2004 Paralympics, to receive the reward money due to him from the government for his Paralympic medal.

Clearly then, the allure did not lie in financial gains. Ask Para athlete, disability rights activist and politician Deepa Malik about her reason to pursue sport, and she puts it thus: 'Disability gave focus to my life and sport gave it direction.' An army daughter and army wife, it is no coincidence that Deepa went on to become India's first female Paralympic medallist in Rio. Having survived a potentially fatal tumour removal which left her paralysed from the chest below, Deepa's life could have taken a very different trajectory, given the many personal and systemic battles she had to fight. She chose to busy herself with advocacy, before eventually making the leap into politics in 2019.

At the Indian Spinal Injury Centre, an Indian-origin volunteer worker opened Deepa's eyes to the prospect of a lifestyle as active as the one she had been used to before her surgery. Seeing videos of him in the gym, seeing him going about his business, leading an active, sporting life, Deepa made it her life's mission to push her activity level beyond just hydrotherapy. She went to her first international competition at the FESPIC Games in 2006.

Being articulate, multilingual and older than the posse of other Indian athletes was of significant advantage to Deepa. She soon became a sort of go-to resource person for the contingent and, in the process, learnt about new directions that her own career could take. The younger athletes pointed out that her height and long hands could be used to her advantage in athletics disciplines. This was followed by the later realization that her career as an international swimmer was not destined to go too far— after all, she was being pitted against amputees who had less lower-body weight to carry in the water, while she had to contend with the prospect of dragging a 5 ft 9 in. frame along, behind her, as dead weight.

In 2009, at the International Wheelchair and Amputee Sports (IWAS) World Games in Bengaluru, Deepa found herself listed (wrongly) on the shot-put list, slated to compete in a sport she had never tried her hand at. With no background on how to throw, the instinctive sportswoman landed the bronze medal by throwing purely using her gut, and subsequently found herself well and truly ensconced in the world of international Para sport.

Deepa was very much a medal prospect in need of support at the time GoSports Foundation's Para Champions Programme took off in 2015. The need for a separate programme for differently abled athletes was glaring—they faced all the challenges that able-bodied athletes did, and then some. Minimal guidance on how to obtain their classification, the paperwork and requisite medical documentation for this, meagre financial muscle for travel, infrastructural access barriers, lopsided (and to a large extent, non-existent) recognition structures—all these considerations meant that there were huge challenges to be overcome before athletes could be ready for global competition.

We found corporate partners for the programme at a time when the Paralympic Committee of India (PCI) had been derecognized and the need to support Para athletes on their immediate Rio 2016 Paralympic quest was highest. These were large organizations that wanted to contribute to enabling sporting achievement in an inclusive manner through their corporate social responsibility outreach. This meant that eighteen emerging and elite Para athletes could receive immediate support on their quest to make it to Rio.

Some were receiving access to high-performance training stints outside India, cleared under the government-supported TOPS (Target Olympic Podium Scheme). Many still needed access to seemingly simple things, such as funding of their escorts' travel, access to better equipment, funding and guidance in the area of sports science, including a customized nutrition programme, strength and conditioning advice, and injury management, all designed to help elite athletes do what they do best—excel.

Looking back at the long history of India's presence at the Paralympics, the one thing that quickly becomes apparent is that athletes were emerging by dint of sheer perseverance and talent, aided and abetted by many strokes of sheer good fortune, receiving only minimal assistance from the formal ecosystem. Even now, the pace of change on the ground is glacial. However, nothing was ever achieved by sitting back and complaining, and we are fortunate to be part of a team that believes in being the force for change and putting in the hard yards to see the needle move. We'd like to elaborate on this by telling you the story of the Rio 2016 Paralympics, as experienced by Deepthi who was at the Games and supporting athletes on behalf of GoSports Foundation.

It all came together for us at Rio; eleven from our Para Champions Programme had qualified for the mega-event. Once I got there though, the ground reality shook me. There was literally no Indian media covering the events, the stories of our heroes were destined to be lost in all the mainstream content back home.

The media and sport-loving population was still fixated on how the able-bodied contingent had, only a fortnight previously, brought back just two Olympic medals. Our team chose to make the most of this opportunity. I was on ground and could easily be the mouthpiece relaying our champions' achievements back home. Sure, I did not have accreditation, but I eventually met a kind media director who, puzzled by the fact that multiple Indian athletes were coming to the gate of the Village to meet with a strange lady, gave me a pass to enter the Village. I will forever be indebted to him for this simple act of kindness.

Back home, the stage was set for this event to be more special than previous editions. Our principal partners, IndusInd Bank, created an anthem to celebrate the achievements of Para athletes. Titled 'Jeet Ka Halla' and released to perfect timing just before the Games, it went viral. Our associate partners, Sony Pictures Networks, for the first time in India, acquired the rights to broadcast the highlights of the Indian Paralympics to audiences back home.

What followed over the next fortnight is a blur and holds a touch of the surreal for me. I walked, ran, commuted huge distances to be present at the events where our athletes were. When they began performing—and boy, did they perform!—I followed them back to the Village and recorded them on my phone. This resulted in videos, albeit amateur ones, which transmitted their unbelievable stories back home. On day two, medals came through the indomitable high jumpers Mariyappan Thangavelu and Varun Bhati. Suddenly, the Indian media descended on my team back home, clamouring for access to the medallists, queuing up for interviews. The other athletes obliged the rising expectations as well—Devendra Jhajharia broke his own twelve-year-old world record and brought home a repeat gold. Deepa Malik—biker, consummate adventurer, and a fierce first-time Paralympian at the age of forty-five—hurled the shot-put to become the first ever Indian female Paralympic medallist.

We had been prepared for the deluge. The team had created Wikipedia profiles of all the Paralympians before the Games began, so that curious fans looking them up would actually obtain meaningful information on these elite athletes. I do not believe that any of us slept more than two–three hours a night through the duration of the event. Medals would come in the dead of night back home in India, and by early morning, the team would prepare and disseminate press releases using the videos and photographs that I would hurriedly click and then send back from my accommodation. Precious memories of a very special time for all of us.

The weeks that followed my return from Rio were rendered more special by the fact that people cared! Central and state governments and federations organized felicitations and announced equal prize money. Our remarkable partners organized warm, heartfelt celebrations and flew the champions down to meet with their staff and share with one and all what their support had enabled. Cricket legend Sachin Tendulkar and his network of well-wishers wanted to do something special for the achievers. We suggested honouring not just the four Rio medallists, but all the nine medallists India has ever had—after all, nobody had done this before. They obliged, and entrusted us with the task of contacting the medallists, conducting the due diligence, and presenting them with sizeable cash awards. What a privilege for us! Thus began our task of locating Murlikant Petkar (swimming gold, 1972), Bhimrao Kesarkar (javelin silver, 1984), Joginder Singh Bedi (shot-put silver, 1984; now, sadly, deceased) and his family, and the other more recent medallists, and according them long overdue recognition.

While the medallists received plaudits, we celebrated other highlights as well. Archer Pooja, a ragpicker's daughter, had trained on substandard equipment her entire life, but had become the only archer to feature as part of the contingent. Plucky seventeen-year-old javelin thrower Rinku, who had promised us *phod doonga!* ('I'll kill it!'), finished fifth in the javelin F46 event hurling his personal best distance. The future was bright!

The accolades to the athletes were fantastic and unforeseen and have provided a significant spark to the Paralympic movement. Multiple organizations are taking notice and providing Indian Para athletes with platforms to voice their opinions, and stages to celebrate their achievements, which will allow them to inspire future generations. To cite a few examples, Para swimmer Niranjan Mukundan was recently named on the *Forbes* 30 Under 30 Asia list, in the entertainment and sports category. Many Para athletes have been awarded and recognized by their respective state governments for their contribution to the sports field and society. Javelin legend Jhajharia became India's first Paralympian to make the cut for India's highest sporting honour when he was awarded the Khel Ratna in early 2018. While multiple Para athletes have been conferred with the Arjuna Award over the years, the Khel Ratna has finally proven to be within grasp for them as well. At the same time, Murlikant was sought out from a quiet retirement and awarded the Padma Shri. His first national honour came close to half a century after his feat in Heidelberg. Better late than never, we say.

The longer the wait, the sweeter the fruit. This could also be the title of Jhajharia's autobiography, if indeed he ever decides to write his incredible life story. It all began for the eight-year-old boy from the Churu district in Rajasthan when he lost an arm after touching a live wire while climbing a tree. He cowered at home in shame, hiding his amputation from the world, before his mother told him that he was not weaker than any other child his age just because he had lost a limb. Self-admittedly, that was the turning point of his life. Not only did the youngster throw off the shackles of embarrassment, emboldened by his parent's supportive words, he trained and trained until he was spotted by a coach who honed his natural throwing talent. He may have had only domestic javelins of questionable quality to train with, but Devendra threw his heart out at every event, until one such throw at the 2004 Paralympics fetched him not just a gold medal, but the world record to boot.

His story does not end there; not even close. The twenty-three-year-old was not satisfied with having attained the pinnacle of his sport in his first Paralympics. He went right back and put his heart and soul into training again, waiting for his event to be included at the Paralympic Games. This did not happen at the Beijing Paralympics in 2008, nor at London 2012. Devendra waited for a full three Paralympic cycles, until he could take to the field again in 2016, as a thirty-five-year-old man, now with a family and two children he had not fully gotten to know yet, spending most of the year away from home.

He had a promise to keep. On the phone from distant Finland, a couple of months before his Rio outing, he promised his daughter that he would bring back the gold medal. In fact, the family was united in their promises; in exchange for Devendra bringing home the highest accolade in the sporting world, his daughter had vowed to top her kindergarten class, while his wife had committed to losing 10 kg.

The event commentator's words best capture Devendra's exploits in Rio:

He's the world record holder . . . OH, HE'S THE WORLD RECORD BREAKER!! It stood for twelve years from his Athens gold, and Devendra sends it out to new horizons!!! It's gone well beyond 62 metres, by a long way, look at that! Sensational throw![1]

And, just like that, his long wait and unflinching dedication had paid off, and Devendra was a Paralympic champion, twice over. In 2017, the story of India's indigenous hero Devendra was included as a chapter in class-seven textbooks in Rajasthan. Twelve-year-olds in the state, at the peak of their formative years, are now learning about the boy whose parent taught him that playing sport was the appropriate way of proving that he was physically as 'able' as they come. There are already boys and girls out there who have been inspired to pick up sport because they read the story of the boy who refused to hide away and the man who refused to give up.

Fast-forward to the present and there is still a naivety to Para sport in India. Look past the obvious state of disrepair, and a scent of distinct possibility and transformation is noticeable. At first glance, there are just twelve medals (four gold, four silver, four bronze) to show over a long Paralympic history. Our largest contingent ever might have been out in full force at the Games in 2016, but it comprised all of nineteen people. To put that in perspective: the Chinese contingent of 327 occupied two entire towers at the Athletes' Village. The Indian contingent barely took up two floors of one building. Blink, and you would have missed our athletes at the opening ceremony—sandwiched somewhere between the Hungarian and the Indonesian contingents.

Change has taken long to seep into the ecosystem. The vicious cycle of apathy–demotivation–dropout has slowly begun to change. Gradually, the cycle of dearth of sponsorship, interest and insufficient funding is being disrupted. Since 2016, Paralympians have an increased visibility on television shows and platforms that allow them to share their stories with millions of viewers. With corporates directing their social responsibility funding towards the support of many such athletes, the government working on promotional schemes and a professional support system coming in, there is hope that societal barriers will eventually crumble and absorb differently abled athletes into the mainstream.

The time is right to groom a contingent that is truly representative of the talent that is inherent in India. Multiple stakeholders involved in the process—the sports ministry, federations, educational institutions, corporates, private organizations and individual well-wishers—need to come together in scripting this change. A strengthened Paralympic movement would not only have self-affirming consequences for India in world sport, but also mainstream the differently abled and result in a better integrated society. The change in sporting infrastructure wrought by this would inevitably lead to increased visibility and much deserved equal recognition for differently abled athletes.

The movement has gained in momentum and the discourse has matured, and yet, there remains much to be done. One can't help feeling that just the first few lines of India's Paralympic story have been written.

The authors would like to offer grateful thanks to Apratim Ray and Shripoorna Purohit for research assistance and other support provided in relation to this piece.

go!

Neeru Bhatia's innings as a sports reporter was not accidental but out of choice. Her journey started in 1996 and, since then, it has been a roller-coaster ride—mostly thrilling, and occasionally dour, getting to follow the action both on and off the field from a vantage point. Neeru has had the opportunity to report on almost all sports at home and away from home. But more than just watching and reporting sports news, hers has been a journey of learning about life, sports and sportspersons, experiencing the thrill of high-profile, glitzy international tournaments, watching athletes win, lose, cry and rejoice. Last but not the least, sports led her to dusty, overcrowded courtrooms, too, where matches of a different kind took place. To her, there has always been something new to discover, convey and learn. Neeru's motto has always been to live and let live and tell a story that must be told.

9

Beyond Ad Hoc-ism: Evaluating India's Sports Governance Conundrum

Neeru Bhatia

There is a bit of history to the history. The year was 2004. Rajyavardhan Rathore, then a serving major in the Indian Army, was returning home with a silver medal from the Athens Olympics. Inside the arrival hall of the Indira Gandhi International Airport, New Delhi, a group of ladies from the family, led by Rathore's mother, Manju, and wife, Gayatri, stood together alongside other male members of the family, army officers and key members of the National Rifle Association of India. The then Union Minister for Youth Affairs and Sports, Sunil Dutt, too, was present. There was pin-drop silence. All eyes were on the escalator that was running empty. The moment Rathore stepped on the escalator to come down into the arrival hall, wearing the Indian Olympic Association's blue blazer, the silver medal draped around his neck, the womenfolk let out a collective sob of happiness. The rest clapped.

Rathore was the lone medal winner that Olympics, as had been the case in the previous few editions. And the oft-repeated question—why India, a nation of a billion people, was unable to win more Olympic medals—echoed loudly yet again.

The now-familiar, quadrennial post mortem of the nation's pathetic show at the Olympics pointed fingers at the ad hoc-ism in sports administration, the lack of transparency and accountability of sports officials and sports federations, a sports ecosystem which gave no results and, most importantly, the glaring absence of a systematic, time-bound, sustained sports policy.

Cut to 11 August 2008. The venue, Beijing. The unprecedented happened. Abhinav Bindra won the gold medal in the men's 10-metre air rifle event. It was historic—he became the first Indian athlete to win an individual gold in India's Olympic history. As expectation turned into reality, watched by millions of Indians on their TV sets, the enormity of it slowly started sinking in. The entire nation went into celebration mode as Bindra arrived to crazy scenes at the New Delhi airport—dhols, garlands, cheers, crowds, TV cameras, the toast of a nation. For days after the victorious return home, Bindra described the euphoria he had unleashed as 'overwhelming, intimidating' in his biography, quite aptly titled *A Shot at History*. For an athlete who preferred the relative anonymity that his chosen sport provided—Olympic athletes came nowhere near their outrageously famous counterparts in cricket at home—he couldn't fathom why, in the days that followed, 'everyone wanted to see the medal', as he wrote in the book.

The celebrations of India winning an Olympic gold medal were yet to die down when more surprisingly good news drifted in from Beijing. Boxer Vijender Singh from Rohtak in nearby Haryana had won a bronze. From the plush farmhouse of the Bindras on the outskirts of Chandigarh to the dusty, narrow lanes which led to the Bhiwani Boxing Club (BBC), the media posse back home in India were working overtime. I remember, while on my way back from the BBC to New Delhi, news started filtering in of wrestler Sushil Kumar likely to win a bronze.

The halfway mandatory stop at a dhaba for tea had people all around discussing Olympics and medals. India was having a fantastic time at the Olympics—entire sets of generations, old and new, had never seen it so good—the hockey golds were a faded memory.

So, what exactly happened between 2004 and 2008, which saw India reaping results at the Summer Games like never before? The 2000 Sydney Olympics, another disaster for India, saw the birth of an idea. Two of India's greatest sporting legends came together to form a platform to enable athletes to be better prepared for important competitions. Olympic Gold Quest—the brainchild of many-time billiards world champion Geet Sethi and former All England Open champion Prakash Padukone— was launched in 2002.

The Mittal Champions Trust emerged in 2005. A trust formed by steel magnate L.N. Mittal, it had on board multiple Grand Slam champion Mahesh Bhupathi. Its model was to fund promising athletes long-term. The idea was to take already established athletes (there weren't that many in 2005) to the next level through experts and different systems than the ones that existed. These included funding of foreign training for athletes, foreign coaches and injury management by specialists.

There was also the already prevailing Centre of Excellence Scheme instituted for elite athletes by the Sports Authority of India (SAI), providing funding for training and exposure through the National Sports Development Fund—a combined fund created by the Government of India wherein contributions by corporates via CSR were matched by the Union government, and the funds disbursed exclusively for elite athletes' preparations.

None of the above-mentioned efforts, however, were ever in complete sync with one another.

Between the 2008 and the 2012 Olympics came the Commonwealth Games (CWG) hosted by India in New Delhi. The narrative before the start of the 2010 Commonwealth Games was mostly about scams, missed deadlines, incomplete infrastructure and last-minute painting and denting jobs.

Away from this, in various SAI campuses across the country, in camps on foreign shores, Indian athletes in various competitions were preparing for the Games at home. The Government of India had allocated a separate budget of Rs 678 crore solely for the training of athletes and state-of-the-art equipment. Foreign coaches were roped in; most importantly, there was palpable pressure on

National Sports Federations (NSFs), the Indian Olympic Association (IOA) and coaches—national and foreign—to deliver medals. Federations and SAI officials and coaches met regularly to review the progress of athletes in the run up to the CWG.

Because, after overshooting the budget by a massive 114 times to an estimated Rs 70,608 crore, Indians as hosts could not end up as also-rans in competitions. People witnessed, first-hand, sporting success beyond cricket—in sports that wouldn't otherwise occupy mind space or newspaper space except for once every four years. Names such as the Phogat sisters in wrestling, boxing legend and multiple-time world champion M.C. Mary Kom, boxers Akhil Kumar and Vijender Singh and badminton's lone star Saina Nehwal, all single-handedly challenged the South East Asian powerhouses.

Buoyed by the success of the CWG 2010, medal-wise, the then Union Sports Minister Ajay Maken launched Operation Excellence London 2012 (OPEX). Medal prospects and the top ten categories in selected individual disciplines were identified, managed and funded through the National Sports Development Fund (NSDF). This included preparation of national teams with a focus on training camps, national and foreign coaches, equipment support and exposure through competitions abroad woven into a 'time-bound' programme by the SAI. It also included the formation of an apex committee, which included representatives of NSFs, SAI, CII/FICCI, IOA and former Olympians, which would review specific athletes' progress from time to time.

And so, willy-nilly, all systems working simultaneously, not completely in sync, clashed, yet worked, culminating in India's best show ever in terms of number of medals post 1980. India won six medals at the London Olympics, though a gold proved elusive.

However, ad hoc-ism in planning and decision-making has been the bane of Indian sports right through. Post London 2012, a lull in planning was visible. Lethargy in policy initiatives until 2014, up to almost a year after, was obvious. As has been India's second nature, even as government funding for athletes' training continued, the stop-start approach and precious time wasted resulted in India returning with barely two medals in Rio 2016— a bronze won by wrestler Sakshi Malik and silver by badminton player P.V. Sindhu. It was only fair to say that despite government funding for Rio preparations via the Target Olympic Podium Scheme (TOPS), which saw many changes in personnel and structure, a lot of credit for the two medals went to the athletes' individual efforts and, in the case of badminton, a strict, planned programme helmed by badminton legend and national head coach Pullela Gopichand.

Sports being a subject on the State List of the Indian Constitution has also been a serious issue when it comes to development structures. The call to bring it on the Concurrent List has been there for many years but successive governments have failed to come to a consensus on it. The unequal development of sports facilities in the country has also played a big role in holding back sports development. Take the example of Dipa Karmakar—the first Indian gymnast to qualify for the finals at the Olympics, finishing fourth in 2016. Back in her home state of Tripura, in her hometown Agartala, she could not practise the dangerous Produnova vault because the gymnasium there did not have the foam pit to safely land on. That facility was only available at the Indira Gandhi Indoor Stadium in New Delhi. The situation is better now.

~

The CWG 2010 scandal and the public outrage that followed led to the downfall of IOA top boss Suresh Kalmadi and his team on charges of alleged corruption. The immediate fallout of this scandal was the decision to bring in the National Sports Development Bill by then Union minister Ajay Maken. The basis of such a bill was the absence of strict regulation in Indian sports organizations, a lack of transparency in their functioning as well as a lack of professionalism in administration. With all NSFs being almost fully dependent on public funding for their athletes' programmes, coaching, competitions and trips offering exposure, these NSFs were considered to be performing public functions and hence came under the ambit of the Right to Information Act.

The bill had 'too good to be true' written on it from day one. Athletes, sports activists and the media welcomed it. The move was summarily dismissed by sports bosses, particularly politicians cutting across party lines. In April 2011, the Union sports ministry announced the formation of a committee chaired by the former chief justice of the

Punjab and Haryana High Court, Justice Mukul Mudgal, to fine-tune the draft of the National Sports Development Bill. The committee sought views in writing and in person from a wide cross-section of the society—journalists, sports writers, athletes, sports administrators and sports activists, travelling to various cities of the country.

The bill sought to cap the age of elected officials in NSFs at seventy years and sought the inclusion of athletes in the decision-making process. It aimed at making it mandatory for 25 per cent of the membership and voting powers in NSFs to be held by the athletes and put restrictions on the terms of office-bearers—to two terms, each of four years' duration. The draft was based on 'Basic Universal Principles of Good Governance' proposed by the International Olympic Committee (IOC) and endorsed by the Olympic Congress, and it proposed to deal effectively with the cases of sexual harassment of women and child abuse in sports.[1]

The sports bill draft faced the severest of criticism from senior political leaders of the country who were involved in sports administration. The IOA's acting president, V.K. Malhotra, who had headed the Archery Association of India since 1979, slammed the bill. Senior politicians within and outside the government also opposed the bill viciously. Maken, a relatively younger and enthusiastic minister, was up against the old guard of the political system.

On 30 August 2011, in a meeting of the Union Cabinet, the draft National Sports Development Bill was deferred. Then Union Finance Minister Pranab Mukherjee had remarked that this bill would never see the light of day in its format at the time, as most of the UPA allies would never support it. Prime Minister Dr Manmohan Singh, Union Home Minister P. Chidambaram and Mukherjee were the only supporters of Maken and his bill. They suggested that it should not be dismissed outright—Maken was asked to 'rework' the bill.

The sports bill has indeed not seen the light of day ever since, with subsequent governments, too, deciding to put it in cold storage.

The glaring lack of political will to consider sports as a priority is intrinsic to the manner in which the SAI and the Union sports ministry are treated by almost all governments at the Centre. Ad hoc-ism reigns; very often, the SAI is used as a 'parking lot' for officers who use it as a soft posting or are out of favour with the incumbent government. There is a crying need not only for upgradation of coaches in various SAI centres but also for bringing in a dedicated, professional, qualified cadre with domain knowledge of the sport. As for the ministry, located at the end of the ministerial hub called Shastri Bhawan, the portfolio has been the least favourite of many ministers in the past—very few have gladly and willingly accepted the responsibility.

However, the sports ministry still had the revised National Sports Development Code 2011 to fall back on. Codified in the *Gazette of India* in February 2011, it had been ten years since the last code was revised. It had some salient features related to age and tenure norms, submission of annual accounts on time, transparent and timely elections, timely submission of Long-Term Development Plans and the annual calendar to be posted online, transparent selection trials, etc., which were also part of the draft sports bill.

NSFs became signatories to the code, accepting it in toto—but notably, without making the requisite changes in their constitutions. This meant NSFs being hauled to court via multiple PILs made by sports activist-cum-lawyer Rahul Mehra and others on the grounds of violating the Sports Code. The elections of the IOA, All India Football Federation, National Rifle Association of India, Boxing, Archery Association of India, Volleyball, All India Tennis Association, Badminton Association of India and the Wrestling Federation of India have been the subject of litigation from time to time.

The code itself has been a subject of litigation and opposition. In 2015, the Union sports ministry formed a committee headed by Justice C.K. Mahajan (retd) to redraft the code. It was met with opposition from the outset by the IOA, with its secretary general taking an aggressive stand in the very first meeting. 'We will not tolerate any government interference,' he stated, and subsequently, despite an IOA member being part of the committee, no representative from the IOA took part in deliberations. Mehra obtained a stay from the Delhi High Court on the finalization of the report.[2]

The annual recognition of NSFs and government funding is conditional on each one accepting the code and abiding by its terms. During various attempts to update and bring about a fresh code, the Union sports ministry has faced opposition from the IOA and its member federations. Their very first objection is that the code and/or the bill infringes on their autonomy and that the sole 'code' they abide by is the Olympic Charter. Each time, the IOA red-flags the code warning that an IOC suspension might be on the cards. The code and the proposed bill, as the ministry states at their very beginning, reiterate that they follow the basic principles of good governance, autonomy and transparency enshrined in the Olympic Charter.

In 2012, the IOC suspended the IOA due to 'government interference in its elections'.[3] However, there was more to it. The IOA was set to hold elections that included two CWG-scam-tainted office-bearers, which the IOC too had objected to. The IOC even snubbed delegations of the IOA as it consistently held that the elections, wherein these office-bearers emerged victorious, were void.

It took fourteen months, a change in the IOA constitution per IOC directives which barred any official charged with a serious crime from running for elections, an election held under the supervision of the IOC delegation, and assurances from a delegation led by then Union Sports Minister Jitendra Singh and Olympic champion Abhinav Bindra to the IOC for India's return to the Olympic fold.

Since the structure is such that each federation is dependent on the state for funds for coaching, travel, exposure and competition as well as for playing under the Indian national flag, NSFs have no option but to accept the code. From time to time, there have been forays to circumvent the code, such as the attempt of the IOA to bring back tainted officials via the back door in 2016, but the government cracked the whip and instantly derecognized the IOA till it backtracked on its decision.

In July 2016, the Supreme Court order on the Lodha Committee Reforms in cricket was passed. It led to a demand by a host of former athletes to implement the recommendations in other NSFs too. Twenty-eight former Olympians and cricketers moved the Supreme Court for this relief. This case was tagged with the BCCI case and was up for hearing post the Supreme Court order related to the BCCI on 9 August 2018.

After the IOA regained recognition from the government in 2017, the sports ministry announced the formation of yet another committee, this time helmed by Union Sports Secretary Injeti Srinivas, the man who had authored the original code and draft sports bill. It consisted of 2008 Olympic champion Bindra, long jumper Anju Bobby George, badminton legend Prakash Padukone, FIH president Dr Narinder Dhruv Batra and noted lawyer Nandan Kamath. The committee's terms of reference were 'to identify basic universal principles of ethics and good governance based on the IOC Charter of international best practices, Draft National Sports Development Bill, National Sports Development Code of 2011, Supreme Court and High Court judgements'.[4] Mehra moved the Delhi High Court, requesting for a copy of the original draft of the committee's report to be shared with him.[5] The court agreed to his demand and the government was required to provide a copy of the committee's finalized recommendations.

The new code, expected to be stringent in terms of age, tenure and cooling-off periods, and emphasizing professional management and high-performance expert involvement in the NSFs, awaits clearance from the court. Upon the application of the Union sports ministry the proposed new code was withdrawn from the Delhi High Court on the basis that it required stakeholder consultation. The status of a new code remains in limbo and judicial proceedings continue in the high courts and Supreme Court on matters related to the All India Football Federation, the Archery Association of India and other bodies in terms of the applicability of the existing code, the applicability of new judicial precedent and related issues.

~

Even as a non-cricket sporting consciousness was slowly developing in India, cricket, India's numero uno sport, disconnected from the rest of the sporting universe, was chugging along, unchallenged and unaffected. Growing stronger financially and politically, with the governments showing a distinct dislike for interference in a body which had powerful men representing it at state, national and international levels, cricket did not just bond a nation, but also enabled the bonding of party men, rich industrialists and influential lawyers. Most Olympic sports federations were outright dependent on government funding not only for the training of athletes, coaches and competitions, but also for hosting national and international tournaments. Cricket was the lone anomaly in Indian sports which created its own resources, human and financial, ran its own tournaments right down to the district level, and generated profits to match an A-list corporate venture. But more money flowing in also created its own problems. The massive inflow of funds, particularly post IPL, was always going to bring with it more scrutiny.

A few developments led to cricketing and Olympic sports interests hitting common ground. Despite the obvious inequalities between these two sporting ecosystems in India, they had a few similar traits—they were administered amateurishly, often interminably, festering vested interests with little interest in strengthening the game, and more interested in strengthening their hold and clout via the game. For every Vijay Kumar Malhotra who reigned over the Archery Association of India and successfully fought the IOA elections for four decades, there was a Niranjan Shah, former BCCI secretary and vice president, ruler of Saurashtra cricket.

If Suresh Kalmadi, former president of the IOA, had to go down in disgrace over corruption charges, BCCI strongman and president N. Srinivasan faced the Supreme Court's wrath over a conflict of interest and had to be removed by the apex court.

The 2000 match-fixing scandal shook the game worldwide and led to the undoing of top cricketers, including Hansie Cronje and Salim Malik. It exposed the existence of the underworld-bookie mafia and cricketers' nexus which was, till then, a whispered story in press boxes, private parties, team hotels and post-match soirees. In India, a CBI enquiry was initiated, which after months of intense investigation, raids and interrogations, found that Mohammad Azharuddin had allegedly 'fixed' cricket matches with the help of Ajay Jadeja and Nayan Mongia for large sums, and had listed England's Alec Stewart, Australia's Mark Waugh as well as Sri Lanka's Arjuna Ranatunga among the foreign players who were either offered or paid money by bookies.

Importantly, the CBI enquiry noted, there were difficulties in gathering concrete evidence to establish any of these facts in a court of law, which were further accentuated by the lapse of time between the events and the investigation. 'If the matters had been investigated contemporaneously, perhaps far more effective results could have been attained,' the agency noted.[6]

The post-IPL era, beginning 2008, saw the BCCI and its billion-dollar league become a centre of controversies and questions. The next big scam that shook Indian cricket was the 2013 IPL spot-fixing scandal that yet again exposed the bookie-cricketer nexus.

From 2013 to 2016, events unfolded in such a manner that it sent cricket administration into a tailspin. The 2013 IPL spot-fixing scandal was unearthed by the Delhi Police, then helmed by Commissioner Neeraj Kumar. Having learnt their lessons from the 2000 investigation, the cops went looking for tangible proof. Former India medium pacer S. Sreesanth was found guilty of accepting money from bookies, only to be acquitted by a trial court, the charges slapped under MCOCA not found sufficient and hence dropped. The Delhi Police is challenging the decision in the high court. Separate from the criminal proceeding, Sreesanth was also banned by the BCCI for life from formal cricketing activities. In February 2019 the Supreme Court requested the BCCI to review the appropriateness of its life ban after reasonably considering any mitigating circumstances that might exist.

The IPL scam led to an unprecedented shake-up of the most powerful sports body in India. Two Supreme Court-appointed committees led by Justice Mukul Mudgal (retd) and Justice R.M. Lodha (retd) red-flagged the glaring conflicts of interest thriving in Indian cricket and the board. On 18 July 2016, then chief justice of India Justice T.S. Thakur, heading a three-judge bench, brought the curtains down on a two-year-long bitter, hard-fought battle by the BCCI old guard led by ousted president N. Srinivasan. 'Change or perish', pronounced the court, while reading out the 143-page judgement.[7] The order sought to bring in transparency and good governance through a structural and administrative overhaul of the richest cricket board in the world.

Despite being the world's most powerful cricket body, the BCCI also has the dubious distinction of being the only full-member cricket nation in the International Cricket Council (ICC), which does not have a player association. It is now an established fact under the law that the BCCI has a monopoly over the game in India. It has used its financial and authoritarian muscle power to quash any dissent amongst players or officials. The Lodha Committee has sought to change that, giving weightage to players' voices at every level of decision-making. Every time players have raised issues, the BCCI has, in the past, used the lure of one-time benefits, pensions, revised match fees and annual contracts to nip the matter in the bud.

In the wake of the Lodha reforms, only one state association currently boasts a former player as its president—the Cricket Association of Bengal, which is headed by former Indian captain Sourav Ganguly.

The recommendations of the Lodha Committee were accepted in toto by the court. The crucial ones related to age and tenure norms, cooling-off periods between each term of an office-bearer both at centre and state levels, one 'one state, one vote' and, importantly, barring public servants from contesting elections of the cricket board. The day-to-day affairs of the organization were, as per Lodha recommendations, directed to be run by professionals. The committee also recommended a different structure of decision-making and administration, putting limits on the size and make-up of the BCCI apex council.

To ensure its order was abided by, the Supreme Court put a financial squeeze on state associations as well as the BCCI. Undertakings were asked for before approval of any requests for central grants or subsidies by state associations. A four-member Committee of Administrators (COA) led by former Comptroller and Auditor General of India Vinod Rai was put in place to ensure implementation of the reforms. Two BCCI presidents incurred the wrath of the Supreme Court. A stubborn Srinivasan was asked to step down in the wake of his son-in-law Gurunath Meiyappan being found guilty of placing bets with bookies during IPL matches. Post its July 2016 order, Anurag Thakur was removed by the Supreme Court as BCCI president for obstructing implementation of the Lodha reforms, as was Ajay Shirke, secretary of the BCCI.

More than two years have passed since then. The old guard fought tooth and nail. From whisper campaigns to discredit the judges and other pro-reform persons within and without, to blatant, in-your-face refusal to accept reforms—every ploy was tried by those affected by the reforms in Indian cricket to challenge, subvert, obstruct and disregard them.

In spite of both the special leave petition and the curative petition filed by the board against the July 2016 order being rejected, the Supreme Court agreed to give relief to the BCCI by diluting the 'one state, one vote' reform, altered the tenure norm by allowing two consecutive terms to office-bearers in state associations and the BCCI, followed by a three-year cooling-off period instead of one after every tenure. The architect of the BCCI reforms, Justice Lodha, expressed his disappointment over the dilution of key clauses fundamental to the reforms process. Almost two years since the Supreme Court order given by a special bench headed by the former chief justice of India T.S. Thakur pronounced the acceptance of the Lodha Committee reforms, the apex court continues to hear key objections raised by the BCCI. For example, the state associations continue to argue before the Supreme Court under Article 19 (1) (c) of the Constitution of India that the BCCI draft constitution cannot be imposed on the state bodies, which are private membership bodies.

However, despite vehement arguments, the Supreme Court stood firm on one thing that is bound to have a far-reaching ripple effect not just on cricket, but on all sports bodies in India. It retained the age cap of seventy years, disqualified government officials and public servants from contesting elections to sports bodies, and barred individuals from holding an office-bearer's post in more than one sports body. The effort to stop powerful politicians and bureaucrats from holding sway over sports associations for interminable periods has borne fruit. This order takes Indian sports one step closer to much-needed reforms.

A major aspect that was argued and ferociously fought over was the Lodha Committee's belief that the BCCI discharges public function which is subject to the rule of law. In April 2018, the Law Commission of India, on orders of the Supreme Court, submitted a 124-page report to the Union law ministry. It recommended that the BCCI be classified as a 'state' under Article 12 of the Constitution. The report was finalized at a meeting of the full commission in New Delhi. The commission further recommended that not just the board but 'all of its constituent member cricketing associations, provided they fulfil the criteria applicable to BCCI', be brought under the ambit of the 2005 RTI Act.[8]

The match-fixing scandals and other malpractices, such as age fraud and doping, have time and again pointed to the absence of any law in place to govern matters of sporting fraud. The incentives in cricket and Olympic sports in present times are massive. International cricket and IPL pay cheques have made millionaires out of the erstwhile journeymen of cricket—confined to the dull, uncaring, unknown precincts of domestic cricket—and superstars of top-bracket international players representing India. However, more money has also led to more corruption. The IPL 2013 scandal saw the then UPA government bring out a hastily drawn Prevention of Sporting Fraud draft bill; it still gathers dust. Which brings us back to where we began—a scenario where poor sporting structures and deficient management ridden with vested interests time and again lead to malpractices in administration. The perpetrators are emboldened by the absence of stringent law and scrutiny.

And here the twain shall meet—presently, sports bodies, both Olympic- and cricket-related in India, are living in fear of the courts' wrath. Their lone escape route is the power and clout they wield in political circles. Given the glaring lack of political will to reform and professionalize sports in India, combined with ad hoc-ism in decision-making and lack of synergies between stakeholders, results, especially in Olympic sports, continue to be sporadic.

Rathore's silver in Athens had a lot to do with individual effort fuelled by government and army funds; Bindra's golden breakthrough came due to a self-taught process, several hits and misses, self-inflicted pain and trials. The shooting federation woke up to dissipating performances by its top shooters in 2012 and 2016 (in Rio, it drew a complete blank), focusing on its junior programme. Badminton's stupendous success story has been scripted by one man—former All England Open champion and legend Pullela Gopichand. There was no previous programme to base it on; it was his self-devised method to success backed by the Badminton Association of India and the government that has brought about such stupendous results. Saina Nehwal, P.V. Sindhu, Kidambi Srikanth and a host of upcoming talents have made badminton the success story that it is now. But even Gopichand, who had to prove himself, had to create a talented star in Saina first, in order to get access to more and better resources.

An important fact that must be reiterated here is the role of athletes. While massive credit for good results lies duly with the athletes or their immediate support group and coaches, athletes' responsibilities too have increased and accountability is needed with increasing incentives. While the SAI, through its funding and its coaching programmes, plays its due role in the shaping of an athlete's career, the onus is on the athlete and the federations to use these funds systematically, honestly.

Sport in India remains fragmented and can work only if everyone gets on the same page with proper plans in place that they stick to. There are too many people involved with varied interests, and the athletes are always torn between the different entities. These stakeholders ideally should work towards a common goal in tandem. Till that happens, sporting glory will remain sporadic, single chapters of individual success.

Desh Gaurav Sekhri is currently engaged with the Government of India's think tank NITI Aayog, where he leads the legal division and also works extensively in the sports and governance departments. Prior to this, he established and headed the sports law practice at J. Sagar Associates, a national bulge-bracket law firm. He is the author of *Not Out! The Incredible Story of the Indian Premier League*, published by Penguin Random House India, and is currently working on his second book on the business and law of sports in India. A regular columnist, he writes on policy, governance, law and sports for various publications including the *Economic Times* and *Indian Express*, among others. He was a core member of the sports task-force for the Government of the National Capital Territory of Delhi, which drafted the capital's first-ever sports policy. He is admitted to the bar in India and in the state of New York.

10

The Way Forward
for Indian Sports Leagues

Desh Gaurav Sekhri

Introduction

In the simplest of terms, a league is 'a group of teams playing a sport that take part in competitions between each other'. Defined thus, a case can easily be made for each of the many sports leagues that have emerged in India over the past decade, enticed and encouraged by the incredible success of the powerhouse Indian Premier League (IPL). When it comes to a formula for leagues, the IPL, which just completed its twelfth season in 2019, has taken conventional wisdom from across the globe and tossed it out of the window.

The evolution of the 'league'

The trailblazing jurisdictions for leagues have traditionally been in North America and Europe, where leagues are imprinted in culture and society. Their duration and engagement is through a large portion of a calendar year, involving the communities and fans of cities in which teams are based. The more popular teams have a global following and, increasingly, an international presence. Seven leagues across the world arguably have the most significant brand awareness and higher revenues than most other leagues. North America's National Football League (NFL), Major League Baseball (MLB), National Basketball Association (NBA), and the National Hockey League (NHL) dominate, although in recent years, soccer (football) has become a contender, with Major League Soccer (MLS) attracting elite players, such as Zlatan Ibrahimovic and now, Wayne Rooney.[1] In Europe, football unarguably dominates, and arguably the most recognized and lucrative football league in the world is the English Premier League (EPL), now shortened to the Premier League (PL), followed by Spain's La Liga. While these are not the only successful leagues in Europe, they eclipse their rivals such as the German Bundesliga, or Italy's Serie A.

In most of the seasons since it began, the IPL has fielded eight teams, playing fourteen matches each over a season consisting of approximately fifty-six matches (regular season), with four matches in the play-offs. The total number of days the league spans has varied between forty-five and fifty. In league terms, this is atypical, but a standard comparison between the IPL and more traditional or 'orthodox' leagues is difficult, given the unique nature of cricket's disproportionately skewed emphasis on international fixtures. The NFL, NBA, NHL and MLB are almost completely skewed towards club competition, where the league duties virtually replace any obligation on players to participate in international fixtures for their respective countries. The same is the case for mixed martial arts (MMA) promotions, such as the Ultimate Fighting Championship (UFC), which is a relative newcomer to the league landscape but is now one of the most successful in recent seasons. For football leagues in Europe or the rest of the world, the clubs versus country obligations are quite clearly set out, and the FIFA rules mandate precedence, priority and availability of players. Despite relatively straight lines with regard to this, there is often uncertainty and angst when it comes to clubs having their star players available for league fixtures if an international commitment is in the offing.

The Story of the IPL

The IPL began in April 2008, and it captured people's imagination instantly. Ten years later, the IPL is bigger and better than ever before, despite an entire gamut of controversies that have engulfed it. In 2018, not only is it still the most lucrative and popular league in India, or T20 cricket league anywhere in the world, it has actually grown from strength to strength. Most recently, its media rights agreement of $2.55 billion with Star India over the five-season period from 2018–22 eclipses any comparable deal for cricket on a 'per day' basis, either of the club or country variety.[2] It is also the eighth most lucrative media rights deal across sports leagues, beating even the NHL.[3] Especially impressive was that the media-rights deal transpired during what was arguably the most uncertain period for Indian cricket, as the prospect of it being regulated by the Supreme Court of India loomed large. In fact, despite the expected turbulence, the brand value of the league actually witnessed a 26 per cent increase, up to $5.3 billion in 2017 from $4.2 billion[4] the previous year. And the IPL wasn't even the first domestic T20 cricket league conceived. That honour belonged to the Indian Cricket League (ICL). Conceptualized by the Essel Group, the ICL could well have been the ultimate success story rather than the IPL. But, by virtue of sanctions, limited access to playing grounds, mass exits by players, a slump in revenues, and being deemed an 'unofficial' cricket league, it couldn't stay afloat. The IPL, of course, had a different trajectory altogether.

The IPL follows no real precedent of international sports leagues. There are justifiable reasons for this. The packed international calendar, increasing competition from T20 leagues across the world, and the ICC's reluctance to grant the IPL a place in the schedule means that there is only a short window of forty-five to sixty days in a year for the IPL to be held, and even within that window, there are international fixtures for countries other than India. Next, resources for creating infrastructure are lacking, and a window as short as the IPL's may not be cost-effective in terms of building a stadium. For the time being, other sports leagues are too small or not revenue-positive enough to consider sharing the cost of a multisport stadium, so even synergies are difficult to come by. Also, by allowing private stadiums to be developed by teams, the Board of Control for Cricket in India (BCCI) risks alienating the relevant state associations who would see a significant decline in the revenues that they receive for the temporary leasing out of the home stadiums to the IPL franchises. Lastly, the IPL follows a different set of rules than almost any other league in the world, simply because for the last decade and probably beyond, it can.

The original model was simple: revenue was generated primarily during the tournament season, and the chief revenue streams were from broadcasting rights, central and local sponsorships, and to a far lesser extent, from gate revenue and associated events and promotions surrounding the actual matches. No team possessed tangible, quantifiable assets that merited their prices ($67 million–$111.9 million), and it was expected that the league would manage to raise enough sponsorship and broadcast revenue to cover the operating costs of the teams, while a certain amount of the cost of the team would be written off as marketing expenditure/trade-offs for the huge exposure and publicity that the teams/team owners would receive. With the lucrative media-rights deal and increasing sponsor engagement, more will need to be done throughout the year to ensure franchises can build viable and sellable entities beyond just the sixty-day window. Eventually, there is sure to be a move towards year-round verticals and enhanced revenue opportunities for the franchises.

The rise of Indian sports leagues in the shadow of the IPL

The ripple effect of the IPL's success cascaded into virtually every other sport, led by promoters teaming up with national federations. Of these, two have been relatively successful despite it being early days in the life cycles of leagues in India. The Indian Super League (ISL), football's professional sports league along the lines of the IPL, commenced in 2014, with significant promoter support, and corporate support on the franchise and sponsorship end.[5] The Pro Kabaddi League (PKL), also started in 2014, has been a unique success story, discussed in greater detail in the next section. The remaining leagues, however, have fallen short of sustainability for the organizers, the corporate investors or the sportspersons themselves. Name a sport, and it probably has or has had a league in the past decade.

Pro Kabaddi League (PKL): Raider of the Lost Art

Kabaddi's success at the league level is a combination of several factors. It is a sport popular among the rural strongholds and, more importantly, a sport that cuts across socio-economic barriers. As a sport that would need the financial thrust to make it viable as a career option, corporate support is required, and this support would also have an external social benefit, given kabaddi's relatively humble origins. From the corporate sector's perspective, it was relatively low-risk and low-investment, as compared to sports which have an international presence, and already established stars and celebrity athletes driving the player wages in excess of total earnings of the franchises. In the absence of pre-packaged and pre-existing stars, the ceiling of potential for kabaddi was high.[6] And to the credit of the broadcaster Star and the league owner Mashal Sports (of which Star is now a majority owner), the PKL seized the opportunity. Savvy marketing, modifications to suit television audiences and an organic strategy to seek a sponsorship premium and not negotiating below a sponsorship floor helped build the brand. Today, the PKL is one of the few sports leagues in India where Indian players are commanding fees in excess of Rs 1 crore.[7]

Kabaddi has inherent advantages that keyed its success. It is an indigenous sport that exists mostly because of Indians. When packaged as well as the PKL is, with the right combination of glitz and high-quality production, the concept was earmarked for success. The overarching presence of celebrities was tapped. But the PKL had a genuinely unique product—one that needed little introduction, was relatively low investment and had a media partner in Star India that promoted the event with supreme enthusiasm.

The PKL has premier home-grown talent, a ready audience already existing in regions and pockets of northern India, along with tier-2 and tier-3 city awareness of the sport, coupled with kabaddi not featuring in most multidiscipline international events—all of which make it easier to expand and enhance the league. In 2017, the PKL added four teams to take the total number of teams to twelve. This led to an over-twelve-week league with 138 matches in contrast to the earlier five weeks and sixty matches.[8] In fact, the PKL, more than any other league in India, replicates the North American NFL, MLB or even NBA structure.

ISL: Football as a culture

The ISL took on the mantle of creating an IPL-style league in football with its huge untapped potential, given the following that the PL and La Liga have among Indian viewers. Its challenge was the limited interest in domestic football, given India's relatively low ranking and relevance on the international football stage, and filling the gap between the offering the I-League, All India Football Federation's (AIFF) traditional football league, provided, and where the real demand lay, through international stars of varying vintage. Unlike the IPL, the domestic talent was not wide or deep enough at the time to rival the EPL or other competitors, and the I-League itself had not been a successful on-ground model. For the franchises, although the ticket size for owning a franchise is much lower than an IPL team, there are limiting factors on the costs and revenue end which make this a longer-term viability project than the IPL, which was essentially a plug-and-play model. The need for recruiting international talent for roster stability meant that expenses were significant right out of the gate. Star India being a key promoter for the ISL meant that its marketing and dissemination was sizeable, bringing it into mainstream consciousness, but on the revenue side for a franchise, there is a huge gap, since the revenue model does not include media rights revenues.[9]

The central revenue pool was extremely significant for a start-up league that wasn't called IPL, but gate revenues remained limited, with one club's senior management estimating total season gate receipts to be in the Rs 1 crore range, with just the salaries costing a franchise close to Rs 16 crore for a particular year.[10] The increasing expenses and continuing challenges with viability haven't prevented the league from expanding, adding two more franchises for the 2018–19 season, and renewing the title sponsorship with Hero MotoCorp for a significant mark-up over the original arrangement.[11] This, despite falling attendance in the previous season.[12] There are future challenges that will need to be resolved but might end up helping league football in India in the long run. A unified Indian football league to replace the currently competing structures, with promotion and relegation between ISL and I-League, is the subject of debate, including a 'key recommendation made by consultants appointed by the Asian Football Confederation (AFC) in a confidential report'.[13]

Structures of leagues

Leagues must offer a unique value proposition that builds upon an already popular and successful sport's core offering and attraction, or they must fill in a gap that exists because of a lack of national or international fixtures in that particular sport. Otherwise, they will be susceptible to saturation, and an inability to leverage either revenues or imprints to enhance viewership. Essentially, two factors are critical when it comes to a league structure—firstly, significant participation at the grass-roots and minor-league level to ensure a ready supply of talent and viewership, and secondly, a wide window of three to nine months annually in which to conduct the league each year. This makes the success of the IPL even more astounding, given that it has been able to achieve NFL and PL-rivalling broadcast deals and valuations on a pro rata basis despite the absence of the latter criterion.

League-first culture: pros and cons

A league-first sporting culture in India has its pros and cons. The three overarching pros are:

a) The visibility and exposure the sport gets from having a league that is broadcast on a leading network, and that has, for the most part, distinct corporate owners who put marketing and dissemination resources behind the league itself.

b) It provides a clear career path to aspiring and elite sportspersons in that sport for earning wages that are significantly higher than they would have earned through traditional sponsorships or organizational support. The IPL is, of course, the perfect example not just for escalated remuneration, but also as a platform for selection to the national squads.[14] Also, if the league does succeed, the visibility and popularity of the standout athletes would be enhanced and, conceivably, so would the financial support base.

c) The creation of a sub-sector for employment opportunities in sports. Leagues help not just players, but also youngsters who want to pursue a career in sports. This is a huge ancillary benefit for what was otherwise a sector with very limited opportunities in sports management, given that most careers would have needed to emanate from the federations/associations, or the limited events that private players could organize. Now, in any given year, there are eight leagues with six to eight teams, meaning roughly and extremely conservatively, 800–1000 non-unique opportunities to be involved directly with a league in some capacity. Ancillary businesses, such as sports marketing, athlete representation and professional services will eventually catch up as well, if in the battle for the survival of the fittest at least five to six leagues remain consistent and viable.

But there are cons as well. First and foremost, the league-first concept tends to gloss over and, at times, completely ignore the grass-roots development of a particular sport. Secondly, the leagues in less lucrative sports tend to not provide wages that would cover an athlete's requirements to support her/his career. Enforcement of basic rights in the less popular leagues is even murkier, including ensuring that wages are paid, or contracts honoured. Thirdly, most leagues in India are glorified tournaments that rarely succeed beyond a few seasons at the most, and at the end of the day, do little to promote or broaden the development within the sport. And therein lies the biggest issue with most leagues that are not the IPL, the ISL or the PKL. Many today are defunct, or have undergone a complete ownership overhaul, or are in their second or third avatars, vulnerable to litigation, and certainly unable to build a long-term strategic vision that would support the owners, the franchises, the personnel and, most importantly, the athletes.

There are also limited long-term branding opportunities for corporates, given the ambiguity regarding naming rights of stadiums, which is a moot point in the first place because no league today owns a stadium. In fact, finding venues for teams is a difficult proposition in and of itself, and frequently a huge cost head.

Corporate engagement in leagues

Ownership of franchises in sports leagues in India has proven to be quite popular, at least optically, with the private sector. Most leagues have a standard format of a central league structure owned by promoters, who then seek corporate owners and partner them with celebrities as co-owners, with varying financial terms and equity allocations. Central sponsorship and team sponsorship are the key revenue models for such leagues, since broadcasting and gate revenues for a majority of the leagues do not contribute much to the top-line, at least in the initial years. Even for relatively established leagues, such as the ISL or the PKL, media rights could be tempered by the fact that the broadcaster also is an owner in the league.[15] Also, unlike international leagues, no tangible infrastructure or assets accrue to the league itself or to any of its franchise owners since stadiums are rented and not owned, even for the IPL or the ISL. This, of course, limits growth potential beyond the 'rights' that are owned by the league or the franchises, but as with the IPL and the PKL, even the 'rights' have significant value and exponential leaps in valuation potential.

While a league-first approach has had its positives, the sports vertical today is flooded with start-up leagues and, unfortunately, a finite sub-set of potential investors or sponsors. There is also significant overlap of stakeholders across leagues, with the same consortium or corporate owning teams in multiple leagues—for example, IQuest Enterprises is the consortium that owns the Chennai PKL team, the Kerala Blasters in the ISL and the Bengaluru Blasters team, which was recently offloaded from the Premier Badminton League.[16] This is great for synergies and consistent practices from the franchise owners' perspective, but not so much in terms of the increase in the overall number of corporates demanding investable opportunities in leagues.[17] The end result is that many leagues fold shortly after their initial few seasons, and the biggest sufferers then are the sportspersons or personnel who often don't have a plan B. This loops back to how best to protect the rights of those who are the most vulnerable in this structure.

Leagues across sports have limited chances at succeeding, and many simply do not because of the market situation and competition. The IPL actually had a valuable blueprint. It took a phenomenon, surrounded it with what works for Indian entertainment, and improved upon what was time-tested. Novice leagues frequently don't have the baseline ingredients for a successful product and are unable to achieve critical mass soon enough for the promoters or investors. Many also do not have any unique overriding aspect that would allow them to build a value proposition that doesn't merely replicate the IPL or the PKL model without the attraction to investors or audiences that the two leagues have already built up.

But, through the market realities, a few leagues have and will eventually emerge, either through elite home-grown talent, the growing popularity of a particular sport or a well-marketed property that derives and provides value to investors, sponsors, participants and, critically, the audiences.

Governance

Processes

Talent development and a farming system are consistent across almost every mature league in the world. These can be in the form of a direct feeder system such as what the NFL and MLB have, through a complex, extensive and successful collegiate system—the National Collegiate Athletic Association, where all colleges and universities in the US that participate in sports come under. Or, they could be in the form of development teams/training squads, such as the ones the PL, La Liga, NFL and MLB have, where players are tried out and then gradually elevated to the major league squad—a lengthy learning and proving process. Thus, talent-spotting, developing and a gruelling minor league or development farming system are necessary components in sophisticated sports jurisdictions for ensuring the quality, depth and replenishment of superstars that make mature leagues successful.

Having worked on numerous constitutional documents for structuring leagues in their initial years, the challenges that promoters faced were plentiful and consistent. Luke-warm interest from corporates, risk aversion that led to demanding performance floors and individually negotiating franchise documents were components that weighed down promoters in nascent leagues. It inevitably turns into a governance quagmire, and rarely, if ever, due to mal-intent. Simply to get the show on the road meant accommodating and compromising while front-ending expenses for the initial years. The processes simply weren't in place. And then, of course, there was the frequent interplay with the sports federations. Volleyball, hockey, badminton and, of course, the infamous Indian Cricket League—in many respects the precursor to the league culture in India—have had a dual-league controversy that has ended up in court. Hockey, in fact, has its third variant—the Hockey India League, which follows the Indian Hockey Federation-promoted Pro Hockey League and the Nimbus Sports Management-promoted World Series Hockey. Ironically, even the Hockey India League suspended operations for the 2018 season.

Excess supply of league properties and finite demand, limited broadcast space (although digital is now filling the gap) and scarcity of infrastructure available make starting and operating a league a far less glamorous and viable proposition than merely liaising between celebrities and corporates. And that's not an aspect that's going to change in the immediate future.

Player representation

A unique feature of North American leagues is the collective bargaining arrangement, whereby the players are represented by a players' union and aided by professionals to negotiate in bulk the wages, rights and other crucial components of the league with the owners and the office of the commissioner. Football is governed by the FIFA rules on transfer and loans of players. Indian leagues, unless they come under the umbrella of the international sports body that covers the sport, tend to not have detailed directives as to how the players' rights will be protected, ascertained and guaranteed. The Lodha Committee recommendation of forming a players' association at the domestic and IPL levels is still unimplemented. If any aspect of league sport in India needs protecting and regulating, it is the players' rights. This today is a huge gap faced in the league-first culture.

The absence of players' associations, or in some cases, associations that exist but go unrecognized by their national federations, as is the case with the Football Players' Association of India (FPAI), makes the balance of power tip completely to the side of the federations and league operators, which isn't ideal. Many of the issues with representative aspects and governance aspects would be resolved if there were player representation in governing councils on matters such as player allocation, player wages, insurance and contract negotiation/drafting. Until a player representative council or a collective bargaining arrangement is in place at the league level, if not the federation level, it will be difficult to ensure parity, development and stability for athletes who compete in the professional leagues.

Going forward, there could be regulation from the Sports Authority of India or the sports ministry to ensure players in leagues get paid in full. Perhaps this can be handled through the No Objection Certificate that the ministry provides to leagues, and the entire component of the unpaid wages can be placed in an escrow account, and at the conclusion of the league and meeting contractual obligations, the wages of players can be secured and paid. Also to be considered would be incidental benefits, such as insurance and financial planning, to be provided to athletes for protecting their long-term future and those of their families.

Gender equality in leagues

Leagues either exclusively for women or co-ed rosters have seen an increase in recent seasons. There is now a pilot football league for women in place since 2017, which had six teams compete over two weeks, with plans to expand to a regular season. Similarly, a women's league seems to be a possibility for the IPL's expansion plans, but making such leagues a viable and sustainable commercial enterprise will be difficult initially given a smaller talent pool, since development has not been a priority focus for women's sports traditionally. A league in such circumstances won't be a quick fix, but may at least kick-start the possibilities for broader-based career opportunities in women's sports. Co-ed rosters in combat sports and already popular sports, such as badminton, tennis and now table tennis, have fared reasonably well, due in large part to women athletes who are household names in each of these sports. Similarly, the IPL may now look to expand into a women's T20 league, at least in the development phase for the time being until there is enough roster strength for a full-fledged league season.

Auction vs. the Draft and Capacity Utilization

The auction system is problematic and should probably be replaced now with a draft, especially in the IPL. Drafts are a mechanism used by leagues to ensure parity among teams in a systematic manner. A draft will credit merit and remunerate the players on the basis of where they are drafted, and not because of game theory and bidding wars. It will also bring continuity to rosters, adjust for market conditions and allow longer-term strategic planning and developing of talent by franchises. It is also a cleaner way of governing player allocation than an auction. Another initiative which will pay instant dividends could be borrowed from the way both European and North American leagues utilize transfer windows per season. With the large rosters that every team has, many deserving players end up sidelined instead of getting a chance at glory, or missing out because of line-ups that happen to click. Teams also suffer due to unexpected injuries, player unavailability due to national duty or limited talent available in the auction.

While a preseason transfer window has been introduced with extremely limited success, and now a relatively limited 'borrowing' initiative has begun in the IPL, one relatively easy way to improvise is by introducing two transfer and loan windows for teams to either trade players in-season with other teams, or to loan players to other teams that need to strengthen their rosters. By introducing a mid-season loan window, and a loan window right before the play-offs, teams loaning out players will be able to offset costs and add to revenues, while teams borrowing players will be able to salvage and even bolster their seasons by filling gaps and mitigating injuries or the unavailability of players originally on their rosters. This will assist parity and competitiveness along with adding a revenue vertical for teams that have spent on players but are unable to avail their talents due to full rosters. Importantly, it will keep the fans engaged and the players productive in a manner that is efficient and determined by market forces.

The Next Ten Years

The league culture in India has been evolving in the past decade. As with most things to do with leagues, the initiative will have to be taken by the IPL and, to a lesser extent, the PKL and ISL for it to percolate down to the other leagues. The leagues have put quite a few sports on the broadcast and awareness map, but too often without the requisite development at the grass-roots or junior levels. Now is the right time to add value to the league verticals by empowering and enhancing the role of the franchises and giving representation and rights to the players and personnel.

If things evolve as they should, this next decade will go a long way towards creating a bespoke sports culture in India that also results in a broader-based sports ecosystem framework and consistently good performances across a full boutique of disciplines. The IPL has shown it can be done. Now it is for the others to replicate it in a viable manner.

Joy Bhattacharjya is currently the CEO of the PVL, India's first professional volleyball league. Earlier, he was project director for the FIFA U-17 World Cup, which, in October 2017, became the most attended and successful junior tournament in the history of FIFA. Prior to that, he was the team director of the Kolkata Knight Riders. Joy was the head of programming for both the History Channel and National Geographic channel for South Asia and was also ESPN Star Sports' first Indian head of production. His stint in sport television included producing live sport, cricket, football, hockey and many others to the best international specifications. He also created popular franchises like Super Selector, Harsha Online and the ESPN School Quiz Olympiad. He has written on sport for the likes of *India Today*, *Man's World*, *Telegraph* and the *Hindustan Times* and has a regular column on sport for the *Economic Times*.

11

Growth of a Sunrise Industry

Joy Bhattacharjya

To set things in context on Indian sport, I usually like to relate an incident from late 2014, when my Chilean colleague Javier Ceppi and I went to meet the sports ministry officials about the FIFA U-17 World Cup to be held in 2017. The mid-level official we met yawned, scratched himself and then told us that since we were the hosts, India should definitely have two teams playing, India 'A' and India 'B'. Fortunately, Javier's understanding of Hindi was not as good as it later got, so I could quickly hustle him out of the room before he understood. An official with fifteen-odd years' experience in sport thought that a football World Cup could have two Indian teams playing. That is probably a good indication of the quality of personnel currently in the sports industry. And a great reason why we need the best minds we can find for Indian sport.

This piece does not attempt to present an exhaustive list of all the possible career options in Indian sport but, rather, provides a fairly personal snapshot of how the opportunities and needs have changed dramatically and offers a sense of the kind of talent that we'll probably need moving forward.

My first real brush with the sporting profession was in 1996. After a stint in software, writing interminably long COBOL programmes to generate payrolls for coal plants in distant lands, I had decided that media and sport were careers more suited to me. It was in 1996, when I was working for the now defunct Business India Television, that I first heard of Transworld International (TWI), which had its office just above ours. I was introduced to a producer there through a colleague, and found out that they were planning a cricket quiz show for Home TV. They had appointed a statistician to set the questions, but I managed to meet the producer and tried to explain that interesting quiz questions were usually not just about numbers. They went ahead with the statistician, but came right back after their first few episodes. And from being a freelance question setter, I slowly worked my way to becoming the producer of the show. My path was hardly unique. In those days, the Internet had not even hit India, and there were absolutely no search agencies to hire for sports professionals. In the TWI office, all of the staff were literally either walk-ins or recommendations. There was even one staff member whom the head of TWI production had found crying at the foyer of a corporate office as she had not managed to clear a job interview. He hired her on the spot, and for good measure, hired her sister as well a few months later!

In those early days, it was a heady feeling working with sport, specifically Indian cricket and football, but the one question that I would inevitably be asked was, 'Why does a country with a billion people win so little?' And, sadly, the only part of the question that really changed over the next decade or so was that the figure in question changed from a billion people to 1.2 billion people.

If one has to look for an inflection point in Indian sport, it would have to be 2008. Abhinav Bindra's Olympic gold medal was a massive breakthrough. While Leander's amazing bronze in 1996 got us into medal contention after heartbreakingly close calls from Milkha Singh and P.T. Usha, Bindra was the one to reach the pinnacle. And it made a huge difference. Being a medal winner was great— being the best in the world took it a huge step further.

The other revolution in Indian sport came with the start of the IPL in the same year. The event had less to do with cricket, which was already at a fairly high level, and more with the way it was organized and delivered. I remember dealing with a member of the Indian cricket board on a routine matter in the mid-2000s, and my mail was duly downloaded by a secretary, printed out and placed on the gentleman's table. He then dictated an answer, which was typed out, printed and mailed back to us, reaching after a week. In the first week of the IPL, with new challenges every day, I sent a mail to the same organization at 7 p.m. on a clarification regarding player eligibility. I received an acknowledgement within the minute and a detailed note which outlined all possible exceptions to the rule and their interpretation, marked to all the competing franchises within an hour. The IPL brought professionalism to the way Indian sport was run, which was otherwise rarely seen on a concerted basis. And we probably needed that just as much as we need our future stars.

Exactly how important is it to cover sport well? In 2000, we commenced our first session of the ESPN School Quiz Olympiad, with Harsha Bhogle as the host. It was an absolute revelation; we were blown away by how much the class nine and ten kids in the competition knew about international sport. Their knowledge of any sport regularly telecast on cable television was absolutely brilliant. But anything on India beyond cricket, especially women's sport, was an absolute black hole. I remember a particular sequence where a visual of Leeds United footballer Harry Kewell was answered in a flash, with the other two teams distraught at not being able to press their buzzer on time. In the same episode, a picture of Shiny Abraham, one of India's finest athletes, was shown. The first team tried P.T. Usha; the other two did not even have a name to guess.

If there was one reason for that, it was the absolutely appalling coverage of Indian sport on television. The real revolution started there in 1993, when Jagmohan Dalmiya and the Board of Control for Cricket in India (BCCI), tired of being pushed around by Doordarshan, sold the rights for Indian cricket to International Management Group (IMG), with the telecast being produced by TWI, IMG's television arm.

TWI was the first full-fledged sports production company in India, and its initial productions were almost completely crewed by international talent. But, in a year, domestic matches also had to be covered according to the contract, and Indian talent slowly started seeping into the system. The first jobs were in operations and logistics. Indian production managers proved more than capable of actually running the day-to-day operations, including cash flow, transport, catering and other support functions, and had a far better sense of reasonable pricing. The next big input was in two hardcore technical areas, namely cameras and EVS (broadcast equipment). Sports cameramen need very different skills from the kind of cameramen who work on serials or even documentaries. Instead of a great sense of light and framing, what is required is a good reading of the game and extremely high levels of concentration. A cameraman covering a cricket match, whose job is following the ball, has to get it right every time. The standard joke was that unlike a film crew, we couldn't go out there, tap Sachin (Tendulkar) on the back and ask him to hit another six as the first one didn't look great on shot.

What was interesting was that most of the best Indian cameramen who first came into sports television were from Doordarshan, which only goes to show that the talent was always there, it was just a matter of guidance and opportunity. The other large bunch was—surprisingly enough—from the Indian Space Research Organization (ISRO). It had an extremely capable audiovisual team, most of whom became the core of the early TWI productions.

There were a couple of other vital technical functions that needed Indian talent. The first was the EVS operations. A game such as cricket is really a game of replays. After the actual delivery and action is covered, we tend to look at the replays from different angles. The EVS operator's job was to record the action on various recorders and offer it up to the director when he needed it. In the predigital area, they were actually recording and ready to replay off tape on their recorders after every delivery. An amazing skill, and early on, the Indians from Doordarshan were absolute naturals at it. EVS operators now have the advantage of recording on digital, but the very same skills of being totally tuned to the game and having really quick decision-making abilities remain essential.

The final frontiers to become Indian were the director and the producer. The directors/vision mixers were the folks who took the mix of cameras, graphics and replays and decided what to put on air at any point in time. Typically, a big production will have a separate director who instructs the cameras and the EVS, and a vision mixer just to mix, while smaller productions will have one person performing both functions.

The producer is, in effect, the head of a sports production. It is usually the person who decides the flow of the programme and prepares the run-order, an excel sheet that captures the flow of events. While there were a lot of Indian assistant producers, the overall producer was usually from abroad, a trend that continues in the larger sporting broadcasts.

How does one get into television production? For the technical staff, it is still very much a reasonably close circle of freelance talent where newcomers are usually blooded on the smaller 'non-live' events before getting their opportunities on big live events. The producers and directors usually start as vision mixers or assistant producers. While a fair number come from media schools, the vast majority are from all over—sports-crazy software engineers, MBAs, liberal arts students and, in short, just about anyone who dreams about getting into sport and is often prepared to take serious pay cuts to enter their industry of choice.

The Indian sports production industry is poised to explode, given that equipment is getting cheaper and easier to use, and there are far more leagues to cover. But there are two basic issues which will need to be tackled if that growth curve is to really take off. First, the number of women in the industry is a tiny fraction of the total workforce, and most of them are in non-editorial functions, such as production management. That proportion has to change if it is to grow faster. And the other issue is that there seems to be no educational degree or institution that really gives a career path to the business. It is pretty much still as hit-or-miss as it used to be.

The IPL officially began on 18 April 2008, but its first real impact on Indian sport happened a few months earlier. On 24 January that year, the BCCI announced winning bids for the eight IPL franchises. And while the value of the winning bids might have garnered immediate attention, the real game changer was that corporate groups, such as Reliance, United Breweries and GMR, had finally become stakeholders in Indian sport, signalling the first real step towards professionalism.

Two things combined to make the IPL a serious differentiator.

The first was that both the league and the franchises had less than three months to get their act together. That meant that the corporate management teams had to quickly learn and cooperate with the hardcore cricket operations staff to hit the ground running. The lack of time ensured that there was no time to bicker and carve out territories. The first example was probably the auction on 20 February 2008. With just a couple of weeks to prepare, most teams ended up with a mix of analysts, cricket players and coaches to work their way through spending the $5 million allotted. The Kolkata Knight Riders (KKR) team had former Indian captain Sourav Ganguly's and former World Cup-winning Australian coach John Buchanan's inputs, combined with an algorithm designed by senior professors of the Indian Statistical Institute, whereas Mindshare, a media buying giant, was intimately involved with the selection of the Deccan Chargers team. The results were mixed, but the principle was established, and six years later, SAP actually partnered with KKR in creating a Decision Support System for the 2014 IPL auctions, which helped them to a championship. Since then, high-level video analysis and decision support systems have become part and parcel of the IPL auctions. Never again would it be just about a 'gut feeling', not backed by data and analysis.

The other was the standards set in the marketing, logistics and support functions of the league and the teams.

One of the most immediate impacts was the influx of highly trained physiotherapists and trainers who came to the various teams. The likes of Andrew Leipus, John Gloster and Adrian Le Roux had already been associated with the national cricket side, but it was the first time that domestic cricketers got the benefit of top-class physiotherapists and trainers. Interestingly, instead of this hurting the Indian physiotherapists and trainers, it actually helped them by creating a demand and a price line. Another 150-odd cricketers started enjoying the benefits of professional physiotherapy and training, and when they went back to their state teams, they now expected the same level of service and pushed their states and associations to provide it. This slowly percolated to other sports. The IPL came at a time when at least one top football club routinely offered Red Bull to its players as a half-time refresher, and its impact on the health and fitness aspect of every sporting league is one of its biggest boons to Indian sport.

The single-biggest bottleneck in Indian sport is the lack of trained coaches. The truth is that a lot of the coaches trained at the National Institute of Sports (NIS) are taught methodologies that haven't changed from the mid-eighties, and the NIS degrees are not even recognized by many federations. For example, the AIFF uses the norms of the Asian Football Confederation. This means that there is little standardization in the teaching of sport. Looking around at the successful models internationally, there is no doubt that it is up to the sports federations to align with international federations to create a single set of coaching licences that are universally recognized. If that can happen, there will be a huge demand for trained coaches in almost every sport. The standardization of coaching norms and licences could be the single-biggest boon to Indian sport, and will probably also account for the most number of jobs in the industry.

Perhaps the single-most important support profession for Indian sport will be legal. This starts at the very root of the sporting system that we inherited from the British. If one were to look at the constitutions of the various sporting federations, almost every rule is ambiguously phrased or has an escape clause, allowing the decision maker discretionary powers. And that is the power that most federation heads wield to hold on to their posts. The Sports Code is the first step towards a uniform code to which every federation's constitution needs to adhere. However, if cricket is any indication, even a win at the highest level will mean attritional battles right down to the state level. The battle for transparency and clear unambiguous rules is one that will go on for quite a while.

At another level, a lot of smaller federations walk the fine line between autonomy and interference. To allow too much outside interference could make them seriously vulnerable to takeover, often political in nature, and deny them the ability to do their job efficiently. To allow total autonomy would create patriarchs who grimly hold on to power.

While the high-profile battles will be in the courts, the bulk of the real work will be in the framing of constitutions, contracts and agreements, and the removal of all the ambiguity in the current documentation, to allow players and federations the protection that they need to function and focus on their sport.

Aside from being actual players, the most desired jobs in sport have to be presentation and commentary. The story of Harsha Bhogle, an IIM Ahmedabad graduate who gave up a corporate job for sports commentary, has acquired legendary proportions and drives thousands to try their luck at presentation and commentary. At ESPN Star Sports, we devised a show, *Dream Job: Harsha ki Khoj*, that worked on that very premise. Many of the finalists on that show, which returned for a second season, are now commentators and presenters on a variety of sports platforms. The interesting part is that the one most desired position, cricket commentary, is probably closed to anyone who hasn't played international cricket. The reason is that, over the last decade, there have been a lot of international cricketers who have figured that this calling was more lucrative than even their playing days, and could keep them in the public eye as well. Ravi Shastri and Sunil Gavaskar were the first Indian cricketers who looked at commentary as a possible second career, and many more have joined the fold since.

That is not to say that there aren't opportunities in sport. Kabaddi, hockey, badminton and wrestling are just some of the sports that have a huge demand for good commentators, and the number of such leagues is on the rise. What is interesting is that other than one broadcaster, nobody has really invested in training commentators. And therefore, the process of the selection of personnel and the quality of commentary is extremely hit-and-miss.

A finishing school for presenters and commentators is an absolute necessity for Indian sports commentary to take the next step.

One of the real success stories in Indian sport has been the coverage of sport. The early sports magazines, such as *Sportsweek* and *Sportsworld*, and the newspapers had a small core of sports reporters who fought for the right to cover events. Sport was not a glamour beat and not really considered big news. That started to change in the early nineties, and news television brought in a whole new wave of reporters and presenters. The 'democratization' of sports news had its own issues. The old guard of print mostly regarded the sports television fraternity as upstarts who did not really know the game well and lived from sound bite to sound bite, while the new wave thought that the old print school had been stuck in the same writing style for decades. In effect, they both did each other a favour. Print writing became younger and fresher, and a lot of the television journalists made a genuine effort to learn more about the game. The Internet just added to the mix, allowing a huge cross-section of sports lovers the opportunity to write on the side, hone their skills and even cover events that traditional print and television did not have the bandwidth to cover.

The real story in the last few years has been the quality of coverage outside the banner sports of cricket and football. The 2018 Commonwealth and Asian Games coverage was outstanding. The doyens of Indian sports journalism have smoothly passed the baton to the next wave of writers, and this is the one area of Indian sport that seems to be in very good hands.

One of the other success stories in the last few years has been the sponsorship puzzle. Since the days of Worldtel and Sachin in the mid-nineties, the top Indian cricketers have had lucrative opportunities. However, the real change has manifested in the other sports. Starting with Saina Nehwal and Sania Mirza, and now with P.V. Sindhu and Pankaj Advani, identifying and positioning sportspersons and events, as also finding fits with specific brands, has made the entire sponsorship market less top-heavy. And while cricket still generates the highest rates, there are many sportspersons and leagues that are now able to command a decent value in the market. Player agency and league sponsorship are two of the fastest-growing parts of the sporting profession, and while there is still a lot of trial and error, there is far more structure and method than ever before.

I grew up in the eighties, the second generation of a country that had a glorious and inspiring freedom movement, and then a rude awakening to starting off as a third-world nation. Our grandparents had dreams of building a great India, but most of our parents just wanted us to have a steady job and, if possible, a green card. For the vast middle-class majority, sport was regarded as a distraction from the essential business of clearing entrance examinations. If it's any consolation, that's no longer as prevalent as before, and many of my generation have got over the obsession surrounding the three or four chosen 'safe' professions. It's much easier today to project sport as a profession to a parent. I know of NASDAQ-listed CEOs whose children are working their way towards their dreams of becoming professional sportsmen, and surgeons who are delighted that their son wants to become a trainer.

The real challenge is that the compensation in the sports industry has just not kept pace with the level of interest. There are a few reasons for this. The first is that sport was considered a 'volunteer' event, something bureaucrats and army officers or royalty did in their spare time. It was not regarded as a proper job. And even when the stakes became much higher, as in cricket, most important posts were 'honorary', which also meant that no one actually could be held accountable for their actions, no matter how huge the perks were on the side. This continues to be a huge issue, especially in the federations.

The other sad truth is that, with a lot of people really keen to enter the industry, it's easy to pay peanuts and keep a revolving-door policy of fresh recruits who could be replaced whenever they demanded more. This is a fairly prevalent trend.

Another reason is that it's not possible to keep paying well if the returns are not coming in. And right now, most of Indian sport is in investment mode. The few areas in the industry where professionals are being paid are areas such as broadcast, where there are revenue streams and an established professional structure in place.

There are, on average, 150 students who take media and sport as an elective at one of the IIMs. Even if a quarter are keen on making this a profession, there is simply no place for them to make a living, even at a 50 per cent pay cut compared to a standard job. Indian sport is at that stage where public enthusiasm and interest is waiting for the industry to catch up.

It's about time.

Photographer: Ahmed Mohiuddin Saleem

Former All England Champion and current Chief National Badminton Coach, Pullela Gopichand, has been responsible for the emergence of Indian badminton players as a force to reckon with. His work has been recognized by the Government of India through the prestigious Rajiv Gandhi Khel Ratna Award, the Arjuna Award, the Padma Bhushan and the Dronacharya Award. He is on the advisory board of GoSports Foundation, and has guided the conceptualization of its education and athlete-development initiatives.

12

The Extra Half Hour

Pullela Gopichand

Soon after my All England win, I read an article suggesting that I knew I would be the All England champion the day I picked up my racquet for the very first time. The notion is so ridiculous that it still makes me laugh. Nothing could be farther from the truth. Growing up in Hyderabad at the time I did, becoming a state champion was the farthest our dream could go. Badminton players from our state barely used to make it through the first round of the nationals, let alone dream of massive international victories (none of us had even heard of the All England at the time!). If only the author knew how narrowly I had avoided my engineering college seat and how close I had come to becoming a really bad engineer! Steve Jobs speaks in one of his talks about connecting the dots. I heard it a while back and realized that a few dots had indeed connected in my life to place me where I am today.

Like almost everyone else around me, I began my sporting journey by playing cricket on the streets with my friends. My mother, Subbaravamma, pushed me towards badminton. This push stemmed from a dual protective instinct—an instinct to protect me from the sunstroke which I would get every summer as well as the need to protect the glass windows around our house. She clearly had a much wider perspective on 'breakthrough' performances than our cricket ball did. My parents first took me to the tennis courts, but there were too many big cars parked outside. This intimidated my family, who then enrolled me in badminton, which happened to have an empty parking lot! I did not care, it was important for me to be playing something, and badminton would do just as well. My brother had joined a few months earlier, and in 1985, I joined a summer camp with four of my friends.

Surrounded by many others my own age, I realized one day that if all of us were to continue playing the same amount, my competence on court would remain roughly the same as theirs. This rather simplistic thought propelled me to work harder. In practice, this meant that if all of us were expected on court at 6 a.m., I began begging my father to take me to the stadium earlier. I did not want my friends to find out, though, so I would get there by 5.30 a.m. and train half an hour extra, then change my T-shirt before they arrived so that it looked as if I had only just got there myself! In a year or so, following this routine, I began beating all of them and reached the state level. I kept applying the same logic to move up through the ranks— state levels, nationals, right up until my first international event, which I played in 1991. The faces of my competitors had changed—now I was playing the Chinese, the Indonesians, the Malaysians—but the principle remained the same. I learnt very early on that I would need immense amounts of *hard work* to be better than my peers. It helped that I had always been competitive in spirit and was in an environment that saw the sport as more than recreation.

Fate also conspired to push me off the path trodden by most Indians at the time. Being a physics–chemistry–mathematics (PCM) student in classes eleven and twelve, of course, I was supposed to become an engineer. My elder brother was also good at sport—he was the U-15 state champion at the time and I was the runner-up. He attended coaching for the IIT JEE and got a straight entry into the IITs with an all-India rank of 101, brilliant as he was. Thankfully, a year later, when it was my turn, I didn't even manage the pass mark of 45 in the state engineering exam and thus managed to narrowly avoid a seat in an engineering college by the skin of my teeth. Ordinarily, with even a pass mark and all my sports certificates put together, I would have landed a seat. Thankfully, fate intervened in my favour and granted me an additional year to play badminton, and my career was able to progress to the next level.

In 1991, at my first international event in Malaysia, I was the youngest in a contingent of eighteen Indians. By the end of the first day, all of us had lost and were out of the tournament. I remember when we had all gathered that evening to collect our daily allowance of $15, I got up and announced in all my youthful enthusiasm, '*Ye Chinese ko main maarke dikhaaunga* (I'll beat the Chinese one day and show everyone).'

Of course, everyone present there pounced on me.

'*Bachcha hai, bohot uchhal raha hai. Thoda haar jaayega toh jaldi samajh jayega* (He's a child, it's ok. He'll understand soon enough when he starts losing to them).'

Some of the others made an extra effort to put me in my place, saying, '*Bohot dekhe hain tere jaise. Thode din mein tu sudhar jayega, jyada bol mat* (We've seen many others like you. Don't mouth off too much now, you'll soon learn your place).'

Walking out of the room later, I still remember being certain that I would defeat the Chinese and show these other guys. At the time, it was nothing more than childish exuberance, naivety perhaps, but one thing I am proud of is that I carried that spirit with me throughout my career, until the day I retired in 2002. I think it was very important that the enthusiasm I brought into my sporting career stayed with me despite my many losses and setbacks over the years. The kid in me was still alive, asserting, '*Main jeetke dikhaunga* (I'm going to win and show them all).'

On the same subject, around 1998, I remember sitting at a training centre with a bunch of juniors around me announcing yet again, for the millionth time, that we could win. The roles had reversed a bit by then, and this time it was one of the youngsters who got up and retorted that I could keep saying these things, but nothing of the sort was happening anyway—we were still losing and would keep losing. I didn't want to be part of an environment that didn't believe I could win. I wanted to protect my belief that I would be able to pull it off. I moved to the Sports Authority of India (SAI) centre in Bengaluru and trained there for the next few years, and I believe that is when I got my best results in a positive, encouraging atmosphere. It didn't matter that I didn't have the best sparring partners there; I was training with other state-level players, but the *positive attitude* and the belief was what kept me going from strength to strength, despite all the other challenges, hardships and defeats.

A few other important things spurred my career on. In 1994, everything was lining up nicely. I was the junior national champion and also the No. 1 player in the senior category. I had just defeated my then role model and good friend, Dipankar Bhattacharjee. When it came to my aspirations, the sky was the limit and everything seemed possible. At the National Games, I had a freak accident, crashing into my partner on court and ending up with an ACL (anterior cruciate ligament) tear on my left knee. Twenty-odd years ago, sports science in India hadn't reached where it has now, and this basically spelt doom. No player before me in the country had come back from an injury of this magnitude to continue to play singles at the highest level. Everything I had based my dreams on collapsed around me in an instant.

Fortunately for me, I had a fantastic support system to keep me from sinking. Right from my doctor, Dr Ashok Rajgopal, my parents to my coaches—all combined forces to bring me back. I returned to win the Nationals in 1996, then followed that victory up with another surgery on the same knee. The cycle continued for a bit—return to competition, big victories, followed by surgeries. With every surgery, I would go back to the doctor and, eventually, this happened so frequently that I was able to self-diagnose. The last time I went, our conversation was as follows:

Me: Doctor, I have a meniscus tear in my left knee, please let's operate upon it straightaway.

Doctor: How do you know?!

Me: I just do. Please go ahead and do the surgery.

The doctor had to go through the motions; he insisted upon the MRI, which showed us what I knew in my gut anyway—the same meniscus was torn again—and he then operated on the knee. Again.

Between 1998 and 2001, I count myself lucky to have been injury-free and was able to rack up some of the best wins of my career. However, I would count my loss at the Olympics as one of the most important incidents at the time. Growing up, my mother, who had seen the war years, used to quip, 'The first son is for the family, the next one is for the military.' So I grew up with this sense of being predestined to do something for the country. Being in the World Top 10 at the time, this was my chance to show that I could win at the highest level. I had always been considered a little mad when it came to my training routine. Now, with the biggest event of my life looming large on the horizon, I went all out. I got up at 4 a.m., did two hours of yoga, visualization, then on to intense, fantastic training, and got into the shape of my life. I put myself in a state where I simply didn't believe that I could ever fail. I won my first match at the Games, a very physical one, only because I was supremely fit.

Back in my room, though, within an hour, my entire body began hurting. Wherever I touched, it hurt. Three massages on the same day didn't help, neither did anything else. I had developed a fever by the next morning and had no idea what was happening to me. Later on, it hit me that my entire life had been spent training on wooden floors. At the Olympics, we were playing on a concrete floor, and the impact every single time my foot hit the floor during the brutally physical match, sent shock waves up my entire body and made it extremely tender. My Olympics was gone; I lost soon because of the fever. This one took me some time to process. For the next two months, I didn't know what had hit me, and I went around like a zombie. And then one fine day, I woke up to the realization that the basis for all my misery was having had too many expectations. Now, I just wanted to get back out there, train, compete, having entirely exorcized the element of expectations from my mind.

The Asian Games, the Asian Championships medals, some of my biggest wins against formidable opponents, including Taufik Hidayat, and finally the win at the fabled All England—all this happened for me in this late phase of my career. What did I learn? Whatever I had visualized for myself did not happen when I wanted it to happen. I had to dig a little deeper, push myself that extra bit further, for it to finally come to me. Yes, hard work and a positive attitude were necessary for my growth as an athlete, but I had to put in the hard yards and then *stop expecting results* in order to experience my best results.

Around this period, as my losses increased in number and the big wins became fewer, and my knees kept hurting, my thoughts turned gradually to coaching. I had understood the mindset required to become an elite-level player, but my own journey, too, had involved a lot of trial and error. I had to wait until I was twenty-seven years old to experience the high of the All England win. At that stage, when I finally knew *how* to win, my body was calling it quits after years of bearing the brunt of my training load.

I also understood that our early training in India used to be fraught with uncertainties. Would the court be available? Would there be electricity? Would the lights be on? Would the coach be available when we got there? Would the gym be open? Would we be able to do recovery in the pool? Would the track be dug up after a function? Would it be usable for our runs? There were such fundamental, infrastructural challenges to progressing as a sportsperson that by the time we experienced meaningful success, we were already in the sunset of our careers. I am convinced that there were at least ten other players during my time who were absolutely world-class and could have made it big, had it not been for needless systemic hurdles that held them back.

The realization that my playing days were drawing to a close, compounded with a strong desire to ensure that the next generation of shuttlers in India could train optimally from an early age, planted the first seeds for the

Gopichand Academy in my mind. I wanted to ensure that the new batch of players could grow without having to face the unnecessary infrastructural impediments that we had, so that they would come by these life-altering victories much earlier and be able to go much farther than previous generations of Indian shuttlers had ever gone. We went ahead and acquired the land for a one-stop centre for excellence in Hyderabad.

As an active athlete who now wished to coach, I can tell you that this required a complete rethinking of everything I had taken for granted as a player. Suddenly, the tables had turned. From just showing up and putting in my best, I now needed to turn up earlier than everyone else, get there by 4 a.m., line up the shuttles, do other things for my students. I was asked why I couldn't have made an easier choice—why not commentary or writing about sport? These things are especially hard to explain when the results of your work may not be evident immediately. We organized our first camp in 2003 (with a first batch that included now-familiar names such as Saina Nehwal, Parupalli Kashyap, Guru Sai Dutt and P.V. Sindhu), and in 2004, we officially began coaching at the Gachibowli stadium. Luckily, I never thought more than a year or two ahead. Going back, if I had to do it all over again, maybe I would think harder about it, but at the time, my only wish was to set up the academy.

The Gopichand Academy took years to get off the ground, literally. We ran from pillar to post, going to corporates, governments, myriad benefactors. Some corporates clearly indicated that their CSR policy did not align with a project of this sort. Others patted my back and said they believed in me and my abilities, but they could not fund the dream. Having earned a certain stature and recognition as an All England champion, I went from signing autographs and taking pictures with fans, to requesting appointments with decision makers, waiting endlessly outside offices for their time. In 2008, I went to one such office for three consecutive days. Two days in a row, I sat there from 9 a.m. to 7 p.m., waiting for the person to meet me. Any residual ego I may have had was eliminated completely from my system. After the interminable wait, I heard them tell me the words I have not forgotten to this day. 'Gopi, we're really sorry but badminton doesn't have the eyeballs to be a big sport in this country. It's not worth it, you're not going to make it.' This was at a stage when the academy was half-complete—we had some funders, but not enough money to finish the project.

I called up my wife and parents, who had thankfully been 100 per cent supportive of the transition I had made. I sought their permission to go for broke—we had begun with a two-bedroom apartment and then moved into a bigger house. Could we sell the new house and move back to a humbler lodging? They agreed readily. This was the most powerful fillip they could have given to my dream at that stage. Eventually, we only ended up mortgaging and not selling the house, and the loan of Rs 3 crore that we got enabled us to complete the setting up of the academy in 2008.

The academy has come up, and a second one has followed just down the road. Athletes from the centre are travelling around the world, playing the biggest events in world badminton. For the first time, in 2017, Indian badminton had five male singles players within the World Top 20 and two female players within the World Top 10. Also, I can proudly assert that in the time I have been coaching, since 2004, my students have never had to forgo a session because of any of the logistical obstacles I listed earlier. It has been a long journey of immense learning for me, first as an athlete, now as a coach.

To be able to continue along this path and grow as a sporting nation, I strongly believe that coaches of varying skill sets are required to make our system more robust and be able to produce champions consistently. Just as many of us come through the educational system having transitioned from primary to secondary school, from school to college, and so on, there needs to be a similar system of handover in sport—from grass-roots to intermediate to elite coaches. I see the role of coaches at each level as being unique and absolutely fundamental to making for a sustainable and robust sporting ecosystem.

I believe that we need to invest in creating more grass-roots-level coaches, who will inculcate in their wards a love for the sport, pay attention to things like movement, focus on learning, be patient, be able to forgive and move on. Their success rates may not be high, because not everyone they coach will go on to play seriously. Intermediate-level coaches need a vision for what is required from a player aiming to compete at the highest level. They need to be workhorses themselves—it is a different mindset altogether from the grass-roots. Elite-level coaches need to have conviction about the knowledge they pass on. They may not be confident about giving advice unless they have experienced the same thing, but at that level, it is about having faith, being open to learning themselves and pointing out aspects that the players themselves cannot see.

Today, when I look back at the coach that I am, I can attest to the fact that every single coach whom I have spent time with has moulded my thought process in various ways. From Hamid Hussain Sir, who inculcated the love of sport in me at the grass-roots level; Arif Sir, my intermediate-level coach, who put in the long hours with me; Prakash (Padukone) Sir, who did not need to expend many words to teach us to dream big and who inspired us with his very presence; Ganguly Prasad Sir, who also emphasized the importance of training and working hard; and my two Chinese coaches, Xiao Ming and Su Yan, who helped me evolve and taught me a lot by virtue of being tough taskmasters. I have learnt a lot from each coach I have been with, and there is no doubt that together, all of them have made me the person I am today.

The way that badminton is played at the highest level is changing almost every three to six months. Kento Momota today plays a very different game from the Lee Chong Weis and the Taufik Hidayats and the Lin Dans of our times. Elite coaches need to keep an open mind and keep learning. In parallel, it is also time to reassess how the coaching setup is structured in India. Elite players, in my view, could actually benefit from having one guru who guides them appropriately and points them in the direction of multiple coaches and experts who would help further their careers, rather than just having the one coach who works with them.

Coaches at all these levels are equally important, and they all need to be rewarded proportionately. They should no longer be subject to the whims of associations, parents, the media, the judiciary. For someone wanting to become a coach, I can only say that they need to be prepared for a path that is not clear and well-structured. Results will not come easily—they will need to work from scratch. My dream is to work to put in place a system that is coach-led and athlete-centric. Athletes will continue to have their comfort zones, but growth can only happen when they push their limits. And for this, they need coaches who will see things they cannot, and push them out of their comfort zones in order for them to evolve.

Coaches are at the core of a nation's sporting growth, but I also believe that an overall holistic view of sporting development needs to be taken. The bottom of the pyramid is as important as the middle and the top. If we build a system that purely focuses on the top of the pyramid in our quest to create more champions, we fail in our duty as a society to recognize the value of sporting activity as being fundamental to human development. If we do not recognize that all three levels—grass-roots, intermediate and elite—need to be addressed in parallel, and act upon this soon, society will begin to look at sport as a non-starter somewhere down the line. While I am delighted to see champions coming up today, I worry constantly about all those others who face an uncertain future, not being privileged enough to make a living from being successful at their sport.

This has its roots in how sport is taught from the early days and how a person goes on to play it. I feel that our society, unfortunately, seems to have lost its wholesome view of literacy, and today takes it to mean only alphabetical and numerical education. While a classroom education is important, physical literacy seems to have taken a back seat over the last thirty to forty years, and the sooner this is reversed, the better it will be for our nation. Only when we acknowledge sport as being an essential part of an educational curriculum will we work towards putting in place the mechanisms and expertise to bolster this system. Then, we can build on the basic sporting skills acquired to create a broad-based talent funnel which, hopefully, will lead to the generation of more sporting champions.

For me, today, sustainable change is the priority for our ecosystem. There is a lot of positivity and belief that has grown, and we need to now focus on how talent is scouted and identified, how it is honed through multiple stages, how all the stakeholders can collaborate to work towards a common vision, and how some of these journeys of individual excellence can be used to build a template. We need to ensure that new talent keeps coming in from different places, and that our horizons keep expanding. Working in isolation cannot be the way forward. Too many people are doing good work separately; imagine what level of excellence can be produced at every stage by the combined forces of initiatives such as Khelo India, SAI, the Badminton Association of India, schools, NGOs, corporates, leagues, sponsors, employers and more such academies across the country!

Back to the present, though. My statement from my younger years no longer sounds as crazy as it did when I originally made it. In 2014, at the China Open, Saina (Nehwal) won the women's singles and Srikanth (Kidambi) won the men's singles, both defeating Chinese players along the way on their home soil. What a feeling it was to see the tricolour go up and our anthem ring out, in the lion's den! Today's athletes no longer harbour any doubts about being as good as their competitors, even if those competitors come from countries with an illustrious lineage in the sport. Indian badminton teams in the past couple of years have participated in multisport events, including the Olympics, the Commonwealth Games and the Asian Games, and have returned with team and individual medals. It also gives me immense joy that in all this, the academy has produced two World No. 1s—Saina became the first female player to achieve this feat in badminton and, in 2018, Srikanth emulated her by becoming the first Indian male World No. 1 in the modern era. Expectations have turned on their heads, and it almost amuses me to see Sindhu and Saina get massive flak today when they are not able to win big tournaments after having reached tough finals. How things have reversed for Indian badminton!

There may have been a reversal in the state of our sport, but there has been one constant for me through this journey—*my principle of spending just half an hour extra on court.* That half hour that makes all the difference. I have always believed in starting the day early—I used to wake up at 4 a.m. to meditate and gather my thoughts for the day ahead. In my early days as a coach, I would do this and head to the academy for the first session of the day at 5.30 a.m. These days, it is my top students who need individual attention to have the best chance at beating their world-class opponents. As their coach, I now make sure to give them exactly what I myself needed in order to grow as a player—that extra half hour on court, earlier than anyone else.

These are interesting times for Indian sport. My story is by no means the end; it cannot be the one set template for others to follow. The story will only progress if more of us become part of the change, and I am delighted to see that this is happening. It thrills me to see varied people from different backgrounds becoming achievers in sport today. With each stellar performance, they rewrite notions of success for all of us. However, all these champions have one thing in common. Their earnestness and will to succeed is what decides their ultimate path. When we look back on their journeys, the dots certainly connect with the benefit of hindsight. Their grit, infallible determination, a never-say-die attitude, and lots and lots of failures are constants in all their lives. For me, while the victories, on and off court, have been fantastic and enjoyable, I would vouch for the value of my failures in shaping most of what I am today. Every single hardship I had to face as a player or a coach, whether it was infrastructural obstacles, or injuries, or defeats which were hard to take, or hindrances to funding my dream, I am not sure I would have been the same person without having made it through each of these stages. All of these have helped me emotionally, influenced the way I plan and made me the thinking athlete that I was and the thinking coach that I am today. Hardships at every stage certainly ended up forming the most valuable stepping stones that helped me progress and grow on my journey.

To those jubilant young kids today who believe that they can beat the best, I want to say, you are right, and you have already set out on the right track! It will not be easy, but you must keep at it, use every situation to learn and grow, work hard and, as the adage goes, if you want it badly enough, the universe will conspire to make it happen. I certainly stand by you. *Hum jeetke dikhayenge.*

Celebrated as the most technically gifted batsman of his time, Rahul Dravid has more than 12,000 runs in Tests and 10,000 runs in ODI cricket. He was awarded the ICC Player of the Year and Test Player of the Year in 2004. Since retiring in 2012, he has coached the India A and India Under-19 teams and multiple franchises in the IPL. He is on the advisory board of GoSports Foundation and encourages the organization to foster diversity and inclusion through its athlete-support initiatives, while mentoring athletes to cope with the rigours of competing at the highest level.

13

Connecting the Dots in India's Sporting Legacy

Rahul Dravid

I would like to begin this article with a story.

This story begins in Islampur, a small village in Sangli district in Maharashtra, with an apparently friendly wrestling match between the pampered son of a village headman and a twelve-year-old boy. Stunningly, the twelve-year-old wins and his reward is death threats from the villagers, who treat this as an insult to their headman. This forces the twelve-year-old to flee the village straight from the wrestling ring, hopping on to a goods truck with nothing but his winning purse, the then princely sum of Rs 12. Without his parents' knowledge, he is now in Pune and joins the Indian army, where he takes up boxing and plays competitively, being seen as a rising sports star in the army. A few years down the line, he requests a posting in

Kashmir and, soon after, he is part of a regiment staving off enemy fire. He is the target of seven bullets in the 1965 war, being hit on the skull, spine, cheek and thighs, and then having a jeep run over him to add to it all. He also loses his memory and forgets his own name. One day, he falls off his hospital bed and hits his head on the floor. This helps him regain his memory. It is only six years later that his family traces him and comes to visit. Looking at his condition, they refuse to take him back, seeing him as an unmanageable burden. This turn of events motivates the young man to come up with a fancy plan to kill himself. As he lies in wait to execute his plan, he plays a game with his hospital attendant and wins Rs 40,000. This causes a change of heart. He checks himself out of hospital, and takes up competitive sport again. Vijay Merchant hears his story, sponsors his training and Murlikant Petkar goes on to win swimming gold for India at the 1972 Paralympic Games in Heidelberg, Germany, breaking the world record of the time. This was India's first Paralympic gold medal! Murlikant had also participated in three other events at the Games, including the javelin throw, making the finals in all, having also represented the country in table tennis.

When I first read this story in the book *Courage beyond Compare* by Sanjay and Medini Sharma,[1] I could barely comprehend that journey. I promise you I didn't make it up.

Murlikant's story is truly unique and without parallel. The journeys and stories of all our nation's sporting achievers fascinate me. I am humbled when I realize the obstacles and challenges that need to be overcome.

The context to the achievement cannot be forgotten either. All this is happening in an environment that may not always understand how to be supportive or why it is important to encourage athletic achievement. The athletes' journeys, battles and victories may be their own, but to view this phenomenon as just their individual journeys is to lose an opportunity to build a legacy of sport in our country.

This is a subject I am deeply passionate about. As a ten-year-old, I remember being overwhelmed with emotion when Kapil Dev ran back to catch Viv Richards in the 1983 World Cup final. When he lifted the World Cup, I was overjoyed—in part, because I could feel something change within me, and in equal measure, I felt this came as a just reward to my cricket-crazy father who had invested so much emotion and time in this game he loved. So, on the one hand it kicked off a new journey—mine—and was an important part of another, my father's.

It might have been all too much for a ten-year-old to comprehend then, but knowing what I do now, I sometimes wonder what went through the heads of those eleven men during the lunch break as they went out to defend 183 in 60 overs against Clive Lloyd's mighty West Indians. Were they perhaps, somewhere in the back of their minds, empowered with the knowledge that India, with her eight Olympic hockey medals, was capable of winning on the world stage? I would like to think the deeds of Dhyan Chand and those who followed him contributed in some way to the belief that victory was indeed possible.

A couple of decades later, there came a young boy from a small town. He achieved, he overachieved. He won everything there was. He made the country proud. En route to his accomplishments, he put his small town on the world map. Today, if people in Australia and West Indies know about Ranchi, I think it has a lot to do with M.S. Dhoni. Ranchi's economy has grown at a rapid pace. A few years ago, I came across a research report and was amazed to find an economic phenomenon called 'The Dhoni Effect'. It is very different from the 'Dravid Effect', which is cited when anyone scores at less than a run a ball these days. Rajgopal of Ernst & Young has this to say about the former:

> The Dhoni Effect identifies a phenomenon where rapidly growing small towns of India are taking centre stage. This research highlights the growing affluence levels, increased awareness due to media penetration, improved physical connectivity, and significant changes in consumption patterns with high aspiration levels of small-town India that are compelling marketers to take notice.[2]

Today, there are more youngsters from small towns dreaming of and aspiring for great things in different walks of life. To me, this was a journey flagged off by the Dhyan Chands and the many other hockey players who gave us a sporting heritage to be proud of, kept alive by our Kapil Devs and their outrageous aspirations, and brought to their full potential by the likes of M.S. Dhoni.

I must also narrate the story from my days of playing U-19 cricket for India. I love sharing this one. We had two bowlers in the U-19 India team. One, a fast bowler from Uttar Pradesh—he spoke only Hindi. The other bowler—a spinner from Kerala—spoke only Malayalam. Neither of them knew any other language. This was all right while they were bowling—as captain, I used a lot of head-nodding, sign language and my limited Hindi to set their fields. But I will never forget the one game when they happened to come together at the crease while we were batting. In the dressing room, we were in splits, wondering how they were going to manage the business of partnership, calling for runs or sharing the strike. Neither man could understand a word of what the other was saying, and yet, they batted and batted, and put on a 100-run partnership for the last wicket. All the opposition sledging went over their heads and they just had a good time speaking the common language of sport, partnership and the aspiration to do well together.

Isn't it amazing that sport can have such an impact on our nation and its people? When we see sporting magic happen, it is exhilarating and inspiring, and it must motivate us to use the full potential of sport in our nation-building exercise.

Around 2008, I was in the middle of a lean patch. The runs had dried up and I was on the wrong side of thirty—not ideal territory in Indian cricket. I needed to pick myself up. I wanted to. I knew I had at least another couple of years of cricket left in me. Around this time, I watched with glee as Abhinav Bindra shot his way to an Olympic gold in Beijing. I still remember the adrenaline rush that I felt at the time. Watching the Indian flag go up and listening to the national anthem moved me.

Reading Abhinav's autobiography was fascinating for me. I think his story must be read by anyone on the quest for excellence. His obsession with perfection stood out. He did absolutely everything in his power to seek perfection. No compromises, no shortcuts! He had a good team around him who could match his obsession. They made sure everything was perfect, even small things, such as shaving a millimetre off the sole of one of his shoes to achieve the right stance. It had to be perfect, and it was! Abhinav could have easily sat back and enjoyed being good at his sport, but he was able to push himself to be great. He found and took all the support he could get to learn about his art and give it his best shot. Abhinav's achievement emboldened me to give my own career that last push, to dig deep again and do whatever it took, as difficult as it might seem.

His 'no shortcuts, no excuses' approach is something we can all aspire for, in whatever tasks, big or small, that we undertake. The patchwork solutions, the temporary fixes, the cutting corners, the jugaad we are so proud of in our work and our relationships may well get the job done, but does this approach truly make us feel alive, or, for that matter, allow us to live to our full potential and push the boundaries of our capabilities?

If I had a daughter, I would definitely tell her the story of M.C. Mary Kom. I have two young sons, and they too have heard her story from me.

Every time I think of Mary, I am astounded by the way she has defied so many odds to go on and be an Olympic medallist. In her journey, I believe that she has broken down so many barriers for young Indian girls, or for that matter, for anyone fighting the odds. Mary, Sania Mirza, Saina Nehwal, Dipa Karmakar and P.V. Sindhu, among others, have redefined what this generation's girls and their parents think about sport. No doubt they stand on the shoulders of the P.T. Ushas, Shiny Abrahams and M.D. Valsammas, who fought the early battles. As each breaks down these barriers, the next generation watches eagerly.

In 2014, I began working closely with a few of our country's junior athletes who aspire to achieve at the Olympics and Paralympics, through GoSports Foundation. I work with the athletes on their goals and approaches, and the team grants financial scholarships to assist them with their sporting expenses. A couple of years later, I took on the fascinating role of being the coach for the India A and India U-19 cricket teams. I have been very impressed with the poise and confidence with which our young athletes carry themselves, and have learnt a lot from our interactions.

You may ask why I tell the stories of these athletes. To me, these are more than stories, these are dots that are beginning to join to create a larger picture and explain this confidence and poise. Besides those I have mentioned, many others like Leander Paes, Prakash Padukone, Geet Sethi, Pullela Gopichand, 'Vishy' Anand, Sushil Kumar, Pankaj Advani, to name only a few, have permanently changed the narrative of Indian sport. Some are still playing and others are giving back in different capacities. Their achievements are no longer anecdotal, and there are more and more people joining them in support every day.

I have grown up in an environment where the dominant narrative of Indian sporting achievement was—*We can't*. These achievers have fought hard, built on each other's body of work and knowledge, and have today changed the script to—*We can*. Working with the next generation of these achievers, I am constantly amazed to see the long way we have come. The prevailing belief is—*We can and we will*. This self-belief is exhilarating, and yet it needs to be tempered and paired with the requisite skills and attitudes that are essential ingredients of sustained excellence.

We take our confidence in certain sports almost for granted today because our earlier sporting heroes have eaten away at practically every stereotype or excuse one can think of over the years. It is a gift we have been given and the *We can* now needs to feed into an *I can* attitude for every Indian who has the aptitude and desire to weave the fabric of sport into their lives. Whether urban or rural, boy or girl, wealthy or not, able-bodied or not, regardless of region, caste or religion. Talent is agnostic. And aspiration is free.

Just how do we go about delivering the value and joy of 'Sport for All'? I cannot say I have all the answers, but I do have a wish list to get us started.

First, we must continue to support our elite athletes and their journeys. This must be done wholeheartedly and not grudgingly, with a full understanding of the value they bring to us as fellow Indians. Let us be more positive, generous, and give credit where it is due. The pipeline of talent is exciting and each of us can play a role in their success. Ultimately, we all benefit from their progress.

Next, while elite sport sets the standard, it cannot be the be-all and end-all of sports policy and development. The net needs to be widened and systems need to be put in place, so the benefits of these elite achievements can be captured and delivered to all. In my view, while the government continues to support the elite talent, the attention of our sporting federations must be shifted to establishing junior sports systems and facilitating community sport through more accessible public facilities, equipment, coaching and competitions that anyone with an interest can access, sample and adopt. Sport is a public good and there is no reason at all for it to be a privilege of the elite athletes. Federations must work to expand the impact and reach of sports for all.

Third, we need to bring together and integrate the concepts of sport and education. At one end, children must sample sports of different sorts in every school in the country, either as part of their syllabus or in after-school programmes. It is a universal language and a wonderful teacher. At the other end, both elite and community sports require a talented and educated set of facilitators, coaches, support staff and administrators. The time is right to also focus on building the human resources that will support and grow our system. As much as we have seen the impact of the IITs, IIMs and other institutions, sports education must be prioritized through upgrading and building the institutions of sports learning and operating them at world-class levels. This will also give sustainable second-career opportunities to athletes whose careers tend to be short and risky. All in all, this could be a game-changer if executed well.

Fourth, we must focus our programmes on women's participation in sport. The 2011 census told us that we have 270 million girls under twenty-five, comprising 20 per cent of our population. The number would certainly have increased today. The Rio 2016 Olympics were an illustration of the fact that our girls hold the key to our country's future, certainly in sports and—I firmly believe—in other areas as well. They undoubtedly make up a significant portion (if not all) of our influencers, doctors, teachers and mothers, among other things, and will comprise a good percentage of our future leaders as well. They are helping shape what India looks like and what being Indian means. Can we give them the best possible chance of bringing sport into their lives? Can we remove the various barriers that stand in the way of our girls playing sport, helping them to continue playing and achieving sporting success? A deeper understanding of societal barriers is the need of the hour, be it safety, perception, bias or otherwise; these need to be understood with sensitivity and addressed with aggression.

Finally, our sporting universe will not be complete if we do not focus equal attention on those participating in Paralympic or Special Olympic disciplines, whether at the elite or competitive levels. Every Indian truly deserves a chance to enjoy the thrill of sporting achievement, regardless of inherent differences. In 2016, the Indian contingent at the Special Olympics brought back 173 medals and ranked third on the overall medal tally. In the same year, our Paralympics contingent of nineteen brought back India's best-ever haul of four medals, including two golds. It is heartening that we, as a country, are learning to understand

and appreciate the context of these performances better. Over the years, India has produced many an illustrious champion in the world of Para sport, one of whom is Devendra Jhajharia. His exploits with the javelin beggar belief—not only did he land the gold medal with a world record-winning throw at the 2004 Paralympics, he went right back and trained undeterred for twelve whole years— three Paralympic cycles!—before his event was included at the Games again. He took the field as a thirty-five-year-old in 2016, only to better his previous throw and bring back *another* gold medal, with another world record to boot! What a story! He recently became the first-ever Para athlete to be named for India's highest sporting honour, the Khel Ratna. In 2018, Murlikant Petkar—a mere forty-six years after becoming the first Indian Paralympic gold medallist ever—was bestowed with his first-ever national honour, the Padma Shri. I would like the Paralympic and Special Olympics movements to receive special attention from the government, and sustained plaudits and encouragement from all of us.

I would be incredibly happy if the national sports policy takes active steps and our behaviour results in projects that raise the water level on all these fronts.

Before concluding, I would like to share a small story that sums up the way I feel.

In 2014, Kidambi Srikanth, then a young badminton player we had been supporting through GoSports Foundation for some years, shocked the badminton world by beating the legendary Lin Dan in his own den at the China Open to win that tournament. The only other Indian to have beaten 'Super Dan' before this was Srikanth's coach, Pullela Gopichand. The achievement was truly exceptional, but here I would like to include an excerpt of an email received by GoSports Foundation a few days later from a well-wisher. It read:

> Recently I happened to watch your boy Srikanth Kidambi beating Lin Dan. He played with a cool head and showed real international talent. His victory was simply a great achievement . . . Thank you for giving a reason to stand tall in an immigration queue with an Indian passport especially when travelling Far East. God bless.

It fills me with pride to note that the same Srikanth went on to attain the World No. 1 tag in 2018, becoming the first Indian male player to achieve the top spot in his sport in the modern era. His passion for racquet sport may have been sparked by a chance encounter with the freshly crowned All England champion Gopichand, but inspiration has come full circle, and today, children training in badminton academies all over India look up to Srikanth with awe and, even better, a burning desire to emulate his feats! Who would have imagined a decade or two ago that we would have two World No. 1s in Saina and Srikanth in a sport such as badminton?

We are over 1.2 billion Indians, and not all may have passports. Not all may have to stand in immigration queues, as the well-wisher mentioned above did. But every Indian deserves the chance to enjoy sport and sporting achievement.

As I said, the dots are many, they are connecting, and the picture is growing in size and sophistication. In my view, we are well equipped as a people to achieve at sport. We are determined, we are talented, we make do with whatever we have got, we pick ourselves up and fight again. We are proud to be Indian. Let us think back to Murlikant. If he can, we can. You and I can. I believe that we have what it takes to become a great sporting nation. Let us, through the essays in this book, first take stock of the distance that has been covered, and then set our sights on the exciting and challenging road that still lies ahead of us. We must go out, make it happen and live that destiny. I will do my bit and hope each of you will.

Thank you and Jai Hind.

Nandan Kamath loves sport and passionately believes in its power to transform individuals, communities, nations, even the entire world. While not caught up in his lofty dreams and random thoughts, he spends his time as a Bengaluru-based lawyer working with athletes, teams, federations and businesses. He is also managing trustee of GoSports Foundation, a non-profit he co-founded in 2008. Nandan is a graduate of the National Law School of India University, the University of Oxford and Harvard Law School, and was a recipient of the Rhodes Scholarship. He was a national-level junior cricketer and remains most proud of his fielding exploits in the slips.

Epilogue

Nandan Kamath

Excellence is disruptive. It challenges, it inconveniences, it inspires, it demands, it frustrates, it reimagines, it nudges, it alters. Often, it does all these things at once.

The essays in this publication have traced the evolving Indian sports narrative while it is undergoing a fundamental re-crafting. Indian sporting achievements are no longer purely anecdotal, one-off cases. At the same time, excellence itself has not yet been embedded into practices and systems. This means there is some distance to travel before it is institutionalized—where success is an almost inevitable outcome when the talent exists. This puts Indian sport in an interesting place, somewhere between despair and hope, albeit far closer to hope than we have ever been. There is still a long way to go and much work to be done if we are to consolidate the gains we have made. That said, every now and then, it is important to sit back and see just how far we have come. This is not only to check the temperature but also to look back and see what has, and hasn't, worked. Our authors have expertly captured the pushes and pulls, frustrations and jubilations, provided a taste of what has been and a flavour of what might be in the melting pot that is Indian sport.

If not for one man and his relentless pursuit of excellence, we would probably have been in a very different place than where we find ourselves today. This book would certainly have different content, or perhaps, it may not have been compiled at all. As that final shot left Abhinav Bindra's rifle at the 2008 Olympics, it cut through not just the tense air in the shooting range, but also irreversibly changed what it meant to be an Indian athlete. Nobody could say again that Indians were incapable of individual Olympic golds. In breaking down his journey to gold, Abhinav has captured the crazy struggle, the self-doubt and the gruelling mundanity of excellence. Rohit Brijnath has described how the fruits of an athlete's labour are often savoured by others who follow, rather than the athlete himself. In the case of Bindra, an athlete so wedded to process that he was almost entirely detached from results, this outcome might be fitting, even poetic. The ability to change mindsets and beliefs has kept his gold medal alive, outside the Chandigarh cabinet that it physically sits in and inside every Indian athlete's psyche.

Sport creates, sustains and amplifies brands arising out of athletes, products, services and events. But what of the brand of 'sport' itself? Santosh Desai has traced how far the Indian brand story has traversed in recent years, the elements that have given it succour and safe harbour and those that have boosted its journey. It is not just the expectation of the athlete that has changed, but the increasingly globalized and nationalistic Indian expects more, demands more, from the events they attend, the athletes and teams they follow and the products they consume. This shifts the goalposts in numerous extremely positive ways. Many of the essential elements seem to be converging for the 'momentum' to be converted into a 'movement', and as Desai ends his piece, 'for the first time, it does seem that this is not an impossible dream'.

Is an achievement a meaningful achievement if nobody else knows about it? Sharda Ugra's piece has explored the shifting relationship between the athlete and her story. Who gets to tell the story? How is it told? What type of language is used? These are all increasingly dynamic and shifting concepts that have a direct impact on power relations between and among athletes, storytellers and fans. It is probably no coincidence that this shift has coincided with the sharp rise in the number of stories that are being told and the emergence of the confident, self-assured Indian athlete on and off the field. The continued growth of both will be vital to capture if India is to deliver the full social value of sporting achievements to her people.

As the pursuit has gradually shifted from one of leisure and amateur play to the more serious profession of sport, so has the demographic of its participants. This has made for a more vibrant, multicultural and diverse base, as Shivani Naik's piece has demonstrated. The 'single sport' nation is a fast-disappearing concept and athletes from disciplines beyond cricket are building their own long-form stories, and also their legacies. That it is almost impossible to predict which sport India's next sporting icon will come from is a story in itself.

If you were required to pick, from the last decade, just one example of a sport finding its feet almost entirely indigenously, it is unambiguously the story of Indian badminton. Multiple athletes have risen to the top echelons of a sport that had seen only two or three world-class players over the past two generations. Interestingly, the catalyst was a couple of those former players turning to coaching and creating islands of excellence. Abhijeet Kulkarni's piece has traced that progression and Pullela Gopichand's personal account later in the book has given us an insight into the motivations and methods that made it possible to produce in India what it seemed impossible to create anywhere—a world-beating batch of Indian athletes that played as a pack, went deep into the draw at most tournaments worldwide, and won team and individual medals at major multisport events. If any other sport needs a blueprint or inspiration, for that matter, they don't need to look very far afield. Gopichand has also presented his vision for a coach-led sporting ecosystem, to be able to build upon the success that has already come. That badminton has produced a World No. 1 in both men's and women's singles and has two Olympic medals while still having some way to go in systematizing its talent identification and coaching system leaves room for delicious possibilities.

The story of Indian sport would be incomplete if the story of the woman athlete and that of the fan were left untold. Roopa Pai's piece has taken us through both, one as the subject and the other as the lens. The odds overcome by many of these women are stunning and have, without a doubt, impacted not just the world of sport but also the gender narrative in the country. The Indian fan has historically gone searching for Indian sporting successes in a way not dissimilar to the quest for a four-leaf clover. She has now begun receiving just deserts for her patience and fandom, with the prospect of more to come.

Paralympic sport has quietly begun claiming significant attention and space in the public psyche, aided largely by the athletes' achievements. While parity of treatment may still be some distance away, we see many of the walls between 'Para' and 'regular' sport being dismantled, including prize money and eligibility for national awards. Deepthi Bopaiah and Aparna Ravichandran's article has detailed the powerful stories of Paralympians who have overcome numerous obstacles on their journeys to success, and highlighted the systemic changes required for Para sport to claim its rightful place in the mainstream narrative of national sport.

All is not hunky dory in Indian sport and the state of governance of sports falls squarely in this category. Neeru Bhatia has traced the various travails of the regulatory system where the only constant has been how Indian sports bodies have dodged accountability and evaded prudential regulations. This is a vital area which will need to be addressed if the more-than-anecdotal successes are to be converted to systems and protocols. Professionalism and accountability become even more critical as the business of sports converges with sports development, and the lines between various stakeholders and their motivations and interests are blurred. The shift from federations exerting power and claiming ownership of sport to a responsibility-driven approach will instead place the governing body in a position of trusteeship. It is likely this will not happen organically, and 'good' governance will have to be legislated upon. After all, the blockages in the plumbing must be fixed before the water flows freely through the system. India will have to set her house in order before claiming a larger role in global sports governance, an aspiration she must wholeheartedly pursue.

The same year as Bindra's gold, the Indian Premier League started on a meteoric journey upwards, one that few would have predicted at its launch. Its growth showed not only the love for anything cricket but also the latent power of the sports-watching population and the commercial appetite waiting on the sidelines if one could build properties and platforms to reach them. Desh Gaurav Sekhri has traced the prospect of aping this commercial model, which has seemed an attractive model to many others across sports but has also led to the downfall of multiple leagues not built on strong fundamentals. The leagues have, nonetheless, altered the salary structures of athletes and more or less replaced the Nationals in prestige, being organized as high-quality events that are broadcast live, that the best players want to participate in. They might not survive as properties but they have pushed the envelope on player compensation and spectator experience. As a result, Indian sport will never be the same again.

Another outcrop of the private league culture is the growth of allied professions around sport. Joy Bhattacharjya's essay has outlined the various career paths that have opened up in sport, a marked difference from the early days. It is an area that will require far greater emphasis, with education, training and experiential learning being keys to developing people and institutions that carry the knowledge and values required to support the high-achieving Indian athlete of the not-too-distant future.

These may all appear to be disparate stories and themes, but when put together in a publication such as this one, the dots begin to connect, as Rahul Dravid has written. There is clarity of vision and an increasing number of qualified professionals able to deliver progress. This will still require political will and a change in thought processes and beliefs to pull off as a collaborative national project. This publication is an attempt to contribute to those efforts.

Sport has the ability to fundamentally change India. That process has begun, with excellence as the driver. There is much more to do and much more to achieve. But there is great joy in the progress that has been made. At GoSports Foundation, we celebrate this progress and are happy to be active participants in the exciting Indian sports story as it continues to be written, told and built upon. Sports as a national project is an idea whose time has come.

Acknowledgements

This book was born of a desire to document and celebrate the many strides Indian sport has made over the last decade. Quickly, it took on a life of its own, and there are many people to thank for bringing it to fruition.

First and foremost, our gratitude to the wonderful authors of the pieces that make this book. Every one of them was bursting with ideas when approached, as each of their pieces now bears testament. Rohit Brijnath, Santosh Desai, Sharda Ugra, Roopa Pai, Neeru Bhatia, Desh Gaurav Sekhri, Joy Bhattacharjya, Abhijeet Kulkarni, Shivani Naik—getting an insight into your process has been an education for us. Your unique styles, inputs, observations and experiences of the Indian sporting ecosystem have enriched this project. Abhinav Bindra, Pullela Gopichand and Rahul Dravid have been three wonderful torchbearers of the Indian sporting dream. To have all of them write about their professional journeys and visions for Indian sport is a rare honour. Their support as advisers to the GoSports Foundation also continues to inspire and propel us forward. The various pieces in this book are profound, sensitive, humorous, optimistic and realistic—as rich in learnings for the casual fan as for the Indian sports professional.

As with most sports, there are teams and people who work behind the scenes to convert potential into reality. This book would not have been what it is without the meticulous efforts and encouragement of our entire team at GoSports Foundation. Deepthi Bopaiah not only brought her experiences to the piece on Paralympic sports but also guided us at multiple crucial stages. Apratim Ray and Shripoorna Purohit in their roles as editorial assistants were invaluable to the project at various critical stages and have been instrumental in helping us bring the final product to fruition. Shreyas Rao, Kaushik Udupa and Sumanth Nagaraj tirelessly fact-checked, proofread and supported our authors, with Yatin Shriwardhankar pitching in initially and Arnav Jain participating in applying the finishing touches. They were assisted by Suraj Swamy, Vikrant Vishwarupe and our other interns along the way. Shailja Jyotsi contributed in laying out the initial photo-essay. It has been a real team effort. We would also like to extend our grateful thanks to Roshan Gopalakrishna and Nihal Zachariah from LawNK, who were instrumental in helping us on the legal front.

We were able to include the photos and cartoons in the photo essay that is a part of this book thanks entirely to the enthusiastic support of many individuals and organizations who provided and licensed their images to us for use. These include Heinz Reinkemeier, Abhinav

Bindra, the Board of Control for Cricket in India, Pankaj Advani, ChessBase India, Baseline Venture, JSW Sports, IMG Reliance, the Premier Badminton League, Sportz & Live Entertainment Pvt. Ltd, the Badminton Association of India, Prakash Padukone, Jimmy Leivon, Mary Kom Regional Boxing Foundation, the estate of Maya Kamath, Satish Acharya, the Pro Kabaddi League, Mashal Sports Pvt. Ltd, the Indian Super League, Football Sports Development Ltd, Joy Bhattacharjya, the Professional Volleyball League, Adidas, IOS Sports & Entertainment, Prakash Padukone Badminton Academy and Jeremy Lalrinnunga. Photographers Bhavesh Bhati and Dilpreet Sandhu captured beautiful athlete images for us which form part of the photo essay. These images tell stories of their own, while the cartoons by Maya Kamath and Satish Acharya make for impactful tongue-in-cheek comments on Indian sport through the ages.

The role of every single one of our donors, supporters and team members at GoSports Foundation cannot be overstated. Their involvement has fuelled a decade of our work in Indian sport and enables our deep engagement with athletes. Each story of every Indian athlete helps tell and retell Indian sport's story.

We would like to thank our families, friends and loved ones for always stoking our enthusiasm and for their unrelenting support to the project. In particular, our enduring gratitude to Maya, Amarnath, Sandhya, Lila and Ravichandran.

A big thanks also goes out to Roopa Pai for talking about this book at length to all and sundry, and connecting us to Gurveen Chadha at Penguin Random House India. Gurveen has been a delight to work with—prompt, professional and responsive. We would like to thank her and the entire team at Penguin Random House India for taking on this book and for collaborating with us seamlessly and providing insightful inputs, advice and support throughout the process.

The biggest thanks of all go out to our Indian athletes, their coaches, their families and the army of experts and professionals working with them—you inspire and stimulate us through your hard work, love of sport and undying desire to excel. Your stories are constantly scripting a new narrative for Indian sport. Indeed, there were a number of inspiring achievements between the writing and publication of the book, necessitating edits and postscripts wherever possible! We salute your drive, passion and desire to excel.

This book is for all of you.

Notes

Chapter 2: Redefining Possibilities for a Nation: The Medal That Taught India to Believe by Rohit Brijnath

1. Rahul Dravid, personal interview with the author, 2018.
2. Abhinav Bindra and Rohit Brijnath, *A Shot at History: My Obsessive Journey to Olympic Gold* (New Delhi: HarperCollins, 2011).
3. Pullela Gopichand, personal interview with the author, 2018.
4. 'Borg credited with changing tennis', CNN.com, 18 July 2011, http://edition.cnn.com/2011/SPORT/tennis/07/18/tennis.borg.cash.interview/index.html.

Chapter 4: Storytelling in Indian Sport by Sharda Ugra

1. Athletics Federation of India (@afiindia), Twitter post, 11 July 2018, https://twitter.com/afiindia/status/1017247103578460160.
2. Athletics Federation of India (@afiindia), Twitter post, 13 July 2018, https://twitter.com/afiindia/status/1017697699620179968.

3. As described to the author by a senior individual at a national news magazine.
4. Sharda Ugra, 'IOA's faux pas and band-aid', LiveMint, 4 May 2016, https://www.livemint.com/Leisure/eJWdPDpHkE1bmImgx37qiO/IOAs-faux-pas-andbandaid.html.
5. Kamesh Srinivasan, 'Li Du shoots down first gold; Suma finishes last', *The Hindu*, 15 August 2004, https://www.thehindu.com/2004/08/15/stories/2004081501991900.htm.
6. 'Gowda ends lowly eighth at London Olympics', *Times of India*, 9 August 2012, https://timesofindia.indiatimes.com/news/Gowda-ends-lowly-eighth-at-London-Olympics/articleshow/15414131.cms.
7. Shobhaa De (@DeShobhaa), Twitter post, 8 August 2016, https://twitter.com/DeShobhaa/status/762658754152325120.
8. Sharda Ugra, 'Amid the sound of silence, a few brave voices', ESPN.in, 20 April 2018, http://www.espn.in/espn/story/_/id/23242355/amid-sound-silence-brave-voices.
9. Sunil Chhetri (@chetrisunil11), Twitter post, 2 June 2018, https://twitter.com/chetrisunil11/status/1002892448513679361.
10. India_AllSports, Twitter.com, https://twitter.com/India_AllSports.
11. Dept of Sports MYAS (IndiaSports), Twitter.com, https://twitter.com/IndiaSports.
12. They have received some incubation funding now.

Chapter 6: Indian Badminton: From Also-Rans to Champions by Abhijeet Kulkarni

1. Abhijeet Kulkarni, 'Understanding Saina Nehwal's roller-coaster relationship with mentor Gopichand', Scroll.in, 20 October 2017, https://scroll.in/field/849626/

understanding-saina-nehwals-roller-coaster-relationship-with-mentor-gopichand.

Chapter 7: *Baadal Pe Paaon Hai:* A Fan's Journey through the Rise and Rise of the Indian Sportswoman by Roopa Pai

1. 'P T Usha: Against all hurdles', *Times of India*, 9 February 2003, https://timesofindia.indiatimes.com/delhi-times/P-T-Usha-Against-all-hurdles/articleshow/36905376.cms.

2. 'If luck is with Anju she can win a medal', Rediff.com, 18 August 2004, https://www.rediff.com/sports/2004/aug/18oly-shiny.htm.

3. Geetanjali Taragi, 'Madhu Sapre's Miss Universe 1992 Answer Was a "Joke" That Could've Changed Our Fate at Rio 2016', ScoopWhoop, 25 August 2016, https://www.scoopwhoop.com/Madhu-Sapre-Miss-Universe-Answer-Makes-Sense-Now/#.cevklwtlo.

4. 'S(up)porting Sport', http://www.thealternative.in/lifestyle/supporting-sport/?print=print.

5. 'Women hockey players receive grants', *Times of India*, 23 January 2010, https://timesofindia.indiatimes.com/top-stories/Women-hockey-players-receive-grants/articleshow/5493130.cms.

6. Shantanu Srivastava, 'Dipa Karmakar: The quest continues', Yahoo! News, 3 April 2018, https://in.news.yahoo.com/dipa-karmakar-quest-continues-083820416.html.

7. Abhimanyu Mathur, 'Dipa Karmakar: Any actress who can do the Produnova can play me', *Times of India*, 26 August 2016, https://timesofindia.indiatimes.com/sports/off-the-field/Dipa-Karmakar-Any-actress-who-can-do-the-Produnova-can-play-me/articleshow/53858788.cms.

Chapter 8: The Indian Paralympic Story Comes of Age by
Deepthi Bopaiah and Aparna Ravichandran

1. Vinayakk Mohanarangan, 'No Coverage, No Journalists,
    No Fans: Champion Devendra Shows Why Paralympians
    Deserve More', ScoopWhoop, 14 September 2016, https://
    www.scoopwhoop.com/No-Coverage-No-Journalists-No-
    Fans-Champion-Devendra-Shows-Why-Paralympians-
    Deserve-More/#.uhvyckkve.

Chapter 9: Beyond Ad Hoc-ism: Evaluating India's Sports
Governance Conundrum by Neeru Bhatia

1. 'Govt. suggests Act to regulate sports bodies', *The Hindu*,
    23 February 2011, https://www.thehindu.com/sport/other-
    sports/Govt.-suggests-Act-to-regulate-sports-bodies/
    article15454836.ece.
2. *Rahul Mehra v. Union of India*, Delhi High Court W.P. (C)
    195/2010.
3. 'Olympics: IOC to discuss double host decision for 2024,
    2028', LiveMint, 10 July 2017, https://www.livemint.com/
    Sports/uqFW70dwDNdWDDVVH5cAAN/Olympics-
    IOC-to-discuss-double-host-decision-for-2024-2028.
    html.
4. 'Abhinav Bindra part of Sports Ministry's committee to
    frame National Sports Development Code', *India Today*,
    5 January 2017, https://www.indiatoday.in/sports/other-
    sports/story/abhinav-bindra-sports-ministry-committee-
    national-sports-development-code-953396-2017-01-05.
5. *Rahul Mehra v. Union of India*.
6. 'Azhar fixed matches, Jadeja, Mongia helped: CBI',
    The Hindu, 1 November 2000, https://www.thehindu.
    com/2000/11/01/stories/01010006.htm.

7. Neeru Bhatia, 'The bitter war: BCCI vs Lodha panel', *Week*, 27 December 2016, https://www.theweek.in/content/archival/news/sports/bcci-vs-lodha-panel.html.

8. Jatin Gandhi, 'BCCI a "state", bring it under RTI ambit: Law Commission', *Hindustan Times*, 19 April 2018, https://www.hindustantimes.com/cricket/law-commission-urges-centre-to-bring-bcci-under-rti-act/story-RX3y9YVg4MpHezQoeNwSbJ.html.

Chapter 10: The Way Forward for Indian Sports Leagues by Desh Gaurav Sekhri

1. Emily Giambalvo, 'Wayne Rooney begins practice with D.C. United: "The quality just comes through"', *Washington Post*, 6 July 2018, https://www.washingtonpost.com/news/soccer-insider/wp/2018/07/06/wayne-rooney-begins-practice-with-d-c-united-the-quality-just-comes-through/?amp;utm_term=.da31c8c42ff7&noredirect=on&utm_term=.9521b46d43d7.

2. Nagraj Gollapudi, 'Star wins IPL rights for US \$2.55 billion', ESPNCricInfo, 4 September 2017, http://www.espncricinfo.com/story/_/id/20570244/star-india-wins-ipl-rights-us-255-billion.

3. 'Biggest media rights deals in sports: Here's where IPL stands', MoneyControl.com, 6 April 2018, https://www.moneycontrol.com/news/business/largest-media-rights-deals-in-sports-heres-where-ipl-stands-2543625.html.

4. Gauri Bhatia, 'India's blockbuster cricket league is beginning to rival even English soccer', CNBC, 17 May 2018, https://www.cnbc.com/2018/04/20/indian-premier-league-india-highly-valued-cricket-tournament.html.

5. Saptarshi Ray, 'How India's ISL became world football's fourth biggest league', *Guardian*, 23 December 2014,

https://www.theguardian.com/football/blog/2014/dec/23/india-super-league-fourth-biggest-league.

6. Manoj Bhagavathula, 'The improbable success of the Pro Kabaddi League', ESPN.in, 28 July 2017, http://www.espn.in/kabaddi/story/_/id/20170469/the-improbable-success-pro-kabaddi-league.

7. Urvi Malvania, 'Day 2: Pro Kabaddi player auction sees Rs 460 million spent', *Business Standard*, 1 June 2018, https://www.business-standard.com/article/companies/day-2-pro-kabaddi-player-auctions-sees-rs-460-million-spent-118060100046_1.html.

8. 'Sporting Nation: In the Making V: India Sports Sponsorship Report 2018', http://bestmediainfo.in/mailer/nl/nl/Sporting_Nation_In_The_Making_V.pdf.

9. Manos Staramopoulos, 'The Indian Super League and future of Indian football', Discovery Football, 3 December 2018, https://www.discoveryfootball.com/the-indian-super-league-and-future-of-indian-football/.

10. Ibid.

11. 'Sporting Nation: In the Making V: India Sports Sponsorship Report 2018'.

12. 'Super League future of Indian soccer despite falling crowds', *USA Today*, 8 February 2018, https://www.usatoday.com/story/sports/soccer/2018/02/08/super-league-future-of-indian-soccer-despite-falling-crowds/110244270/.

13. Debayan Sen, 'AFC-backed report proposes unified league for India', ESPN.in, 29 May 2018, http://www.espn.in/football/india/story/3511815/afc-backed-report-proposes-unified-league-for-india.

14. Ayan Acharya, 'How IPL has been life-changing for talented Indian youngsters', *Sportstar*, 26 January 2018, https://sportstar.thehindu.com/cricket/ipl/how-ipl-been-

life-changing-for-these-talented-indian-youngsters/
article22528834.ece.

15. Gaurav Laghate, 'Pro Kabaddi League franchise owners nervous of Star power', *Economic Times*, 3 December 2018, https://www.google.com/amp/s/m.economictimes.com/industry/media/entertainment/pro-kabaddi-league-franchise-owners-nervous-of-star-power/amp_articleshow/66913573.cms.

16. Manoj Bhagavatula, 'The improbable success of the Pro Kabaddi League', ESPN, 28 July 2017, http://www.espn.in/kabaddi/story/_/id/20170469/the-improbable-success-pro-kabaddi-league.

17. Anu Raghunathan, 'India's Richest Race to Own Sports Teams', *Forbes*, 24 September 2014, https://www.forbes.com/sites/anuraghunathan/2014/09/24/good-sports/#6532c5633474.

Chapter 13: Connecting the Dots in India's Sporting Legacy by Rahul Dravid

1. Sanjay Sharma and Medini Sharma, *Courage beyond Compare: How Ten Athletes Overcame Disability and Adversity to Emerge Champions* (New Delhi: Rupa Publications, 2014).

2. 'Waking up to the Dhoni effect', *Financial Express*, 13 May 2008, https://www.financialexpress.com/archive/waking-up-to-the-dhoni-effect/308825/.

About the Editors

Nandan Kamath and Aparna Ravichandran work with the GoSports Foundation, an independent not-for-profit trust. Established in 2008, it is structured with the belief that sports excellence is a powerful tool to script social change. Its projects are supported through individual and corporate donor contributions as well as corporate social responsibility grants and include athlete- and coach-support programmes, sports education, advocacy and policy initiatives. Rahul Dravid, Abhinav Bindra and Pullela Gopichand serve on its board of advisers. More information about GoSports Foundation is available at www.gosports.in.